Kentucky Core Content Test Preparation for Reading

Teacher's Edition
Grade 3

Harcourt

Orlando   Austin   Chicago   New York   Toronto   London   San Diego

Visit *The Learning Site!*
www.harcourtschool.com

Printed in the United States of America

ISBN 0-15-345910-7

1 2 3 4 5 6 7 8 9 10   073   14 13 12 11 10 09 08 07 06 05

CONTENTS

Teacher's Manual

Student Book

Book 3-1

Theme 1

Theme 2

Introduction

Purpose

Kentucky Core Content Test Preparation for Reading is designed to help Kentucky students in grades 1–6 prepare for the Kentucky Core Content Test.

Getting Started

You may wish to begin by guiding students through the *Tips for Taking a Test* section on pages 3–7. These pages provide support for students in the mechanical aspects of test-taking and give them a solid foundation for what is to follow.

Organization

The book is organized into 6 themes, in the style of the *Trophies* reading program. The reading passages within the book are connected to the selections in *Trophies* by theme or by genre.

- Each of the 30 selections in *Trophies* is represented by a 4-page lesson.
- Each lesson contains 2 reading passages, followed by 6 questions.
- One of the questions uses the Focus Skill taught in the *Trophies* selection.
- Each theme ends with a writing prompt.

The book concludes with a Practice Test.

Test-Taking Tips

Both the passages and the questions are accompanied by boxed *Test-Taking Tips*. These tips provide helpful insights into the organization and structure of standardized tests. They give students strategies for solving difficult questions and for avoiding misunderstandings.

Teacher's Edition

The Teacher's Edition for this book also includes:

- a **Student Profile** for recording students' scores;
- an **Item Analysis** that lists correlations to Kentucky Core Content Test.

SUPPORT FOR WRITING

Use this rubric to assess students' writing.

Score of 4	The composition • is clearly organized and has a strong introduction and conclusion • includes examples and details that elaborate on the central idea • uses specific words that give readers a clear picture, uses different kinds of sentences, and reflects the author's own voice • uses correct capitalization, punctuation, and spelling, and all sentences are correctly written
Score of 3	The composition • is clearly organized and includes an introduction and conclusion, although they may not be strong • includes some examples and details that elaborate on the central idea but also uses some vague words and awkward sentences • uses correct capitalization, punctuation, and spelling most of the time, though there are some errors
Score of 2	The composition • is not clearly organized ideas around a central point, or strays from the topic • includes little or no elaboration • uses few precise words and little sentence variety • includes many errors in spelling, capitalization, and sentence structure
Score of 1	The composition • shows little organization and jumps from point to point without any central idea • includes no examples or details to elaborate the ideas • uses awkward sentences and poor word choices • includes many errors in spelling, capitalization, punctuation, and sentence structure

Kentucky General Scoring Guide
(Grade 4 and Grade 5)

SCORE POINT 4	• You follow all directions and finish all parts of the question. • You are able to answer the question clearly so that others can understand. • You show that you completely understand the information that is asked about. • You show and/or explain the quickest and best way to get an answer. • You are able to show and explain what you know by using complex examples, by showing connections between ideas and the real world, by comparing different ideas, and/or by showing how the ideas work together.
SCORE POINT 3	• You follow all directions and finish most of the parts of the question. • You are able to answer the question clearly so that others can understand. • You show and/or explain that you understand the big ideas about the question, but there may be a few little mistakes or wrong ideas.
SCORE POINT 2	• You follow some of the directions and finish some parts of the question. • Your answer may not be complete, but it is clear so that others can understand. • You understand only parts of the information to answer the question.
SCORE POINT 1	• You understand only a small part of the information asked for in the question. • You only answer a small part of the question.
SCORE POINT 0	• Your answer is completely wrong or has nothing to do with the question.
Blank	• You did not give any answer at all.

Source: *Section 11 2004–2005 DAC Implementation Guide Appendix H: Kentucky Scoring Guide 536*

Student Profile

Student's Name:			
Teacher's Name:			
Level 3-1		**Score**	**Date**
Theme 1 Reading:	Lesson 1		
	Lesson 2		
	Lesson 3		
	Lesson 4		
	Lesson 5		
Theme 1 Writing:			
Theme 2 Reading:	Lesson 6		
	Lesson 7		
	Lesson 8		
	Lesson 9		
	Lesson 10		
Theme 2 Writing:			
Theme 3 Reading:	Lesson 11		
	Lesson 12		
	Lesson 13		
	Lesson 14		
	Lesson 15		
Theme 3 Writing:			
COMMENTS:			

Student Profile

Student's Name:			
Teacher's Name:			
Level 3-2		**Score**	**Date**
Theme 1 Reading:	Lesson 16		
	Lesson 17		
	Lesson 18		
	Lesson 19		
	Lesson 20		
Theme 1 Writing:			
Theme 2 Reading:	Lesson 21		
	Lesson 22		
	Lesson 23		
	Lesson 24		
	Lesson 25		
Theme 2 Writing:			
Theme 3 Reading:	Lesson 26		
	Lesson 27		
	Lesson 28		
	Lesson 29		
	Lesson 30		
Theme 3 Writing:			
Practice Test:	Reading		
	Writing		

ITEM ANALYSIS

These correlations show the pages in *Kentucky Core Content Test Preparation for Reading* where the Kentucky Core Content Test items are assessed.

READING

STRAND: Reading Skills

TOPIC: Use reading skills to comprehend all types of reading materials.

RD-E-1.0.1 Use word recognition strategies (e.g., phonetic principles, context clues, structural analysis) to determine pronunciations and meanings of words in passages. 9, 13, 17, 22, 57, 65, 82, 87, 97, 109, 145

RD-E-2.0.1 Use word recognition strategies (e.g., phonetic principles, context clues, structural analysis) to determine pronunciations and meanings of words in passages. 39, 105, 114, 134

RD-E-1.0.2 Use knowledge of synonyms, antonyms, homonyms, and compound words for comprehension. 9, 21, 31, 43, 53, 85, 97, 143

RD-E-2.0.2 Use knowledge of synonyms, antonyms, homonyms, and compound words for comprehension. 25, 35, 47, 114, 123

RD-E-4.0.2 Use knowledge of synonyms, antonyms, homonyms, and compound words for comprehension. 61

RD-E-1.0.3 Know that some words have multiple meanings and identify the correct meaning as the word is used. 35, 109

RD-E-1.0.4 Recognize the meaning of a word when a prefix or suffix has been added to a base word. 132, 147

RD-E-4.0.4 Recognize the meaning of a word when a prefix or suffix has been added to a base word. 147

RD-E-1.0.5 Recognize the purpose of capitalization, punctuation, boldface type, italics, and indentations used by the author. 78, 90, 100

RD-E-2.0.5 Recognize the purpose of capitalization, punctuation, boldface type, italics, and indentations used by the author. 112, 113

RD-E-4.0.5 Recognize the purpose of capitalization, punctuation, boldface type, italics, and indentations used by the author. 130

STRAND: Literature

TOPIC: Reads whole texts and excerpts such as short stories, novels, essays, poetry, plays, and scripts representing various historical and cultural perspectives.

RD-E-1.0.6 Explain the meaning of a passage taken from texts appropriate for elementary school students. 9, 17, 31, 65, 75, 118

RD-E-1.0.7 Demonstrate knowledge of the characteristics of fiction, nonfiction, poetry, and plays. 57, 88, 91, 118, 143

RD-E-1.0.8 Describe characters, plot, setting, and problem/solution of a passage. 9, 13, 17, 21, 43, 53, 57, 65, 69, 79, 82, 91, 97, 118, 143, 145, 146, 147

RD-E-1.0.9 Explain a character's actions based on a passage. 13, 17, 69, 79, 82, 87, 91, 97

RD-E-1.0.10 Connect literature to students' lives and real world issues. 17, 57, 65, 82, 87, 109, 145

STRAND: Informational Reading

TOPIC: Read whole texts and excerpts from journals, magazines, newspaper articles, letters, brochures, reference materials, essays, nonfiction books, and electronic texts.

RD-E-2.0.6 Use text features (e.g., pictures, lists, tables, charts, graphs, tables of contents, indexes, glossaries, headings, captions) to understand a passage. 113, 127, 131, 134, 147, 150, 153

RD-E-2.0.7 Identify the organizational pattern in a passage: sequence, cause and effect, and/or comparison and contrast. 25, 35, 39, 101, 113, 123, 127, 131, 147

RD-E-2.0.8 Identify main ideas and details that support them. 25, 35, 39, 47, 101, 113, 123, 127, 134, 147

RD-E-2.0.9 Make predictions and draw conclusions based on what is read. 105, 131, 134

RD-E-2.0.10 Connect the content of a passage to students' lives and/or real world issues. 123

STRAND: Persuasive Reading

TOPIC: Read whole texts and excerpts from magazine and newspaper articles, brochures, letters, proposals, speeches, editorials, electronic texts, essays, opinion columns, and advertisements.

RD-E-3.0.6 Identify an author's opinion about a subject. 131

RD-E-3.0.7 Identify fact and/or opinion. 141

RD-E-3.0.8 Identify information that is supported by fact. 141

STRAND: Practical/Workplace Reading

TOPIC: Reads whole texts and excerpts from materials such as articles, letters, memos, brochures, electronic texts, warranties, recipes, forms, consumer texts, manuals, schedules, and directions.

Grade 3

RD-E-4.0.6 Locate and apply information for authentic purposes. 61

RD-E-4.0.8 Explain why the correct sequence is important. 61

RD-E-4.0.9 Interpret specialized vocabulary (words and terms specific to understanding the content) found in practical/workplace passages. 125

WRITING

STRAND: Writing Criteria WR-E-1

TOPIC: Idea Development WR-E-1.B
Develops and supports main ideas and deepens the audience's understanding.

WR-E-1.B.0.1 Uses logical, justified, and suitable explanation. 101, 139

WR-E-1.B.0.2 Provides relevant elaboration. 51, 73, 101, 122

TOPIC: Organization WR-E-1.C
Creates unity and coherence to accomplish the focused purpose.

WR-E-1.C.0.1 Engages the audience and establishes a context for reading. 29, 51, 54, 73, 95, 117, 139, 152, 155

WR-E-1.C.0.2 Places ideas and support in a meaningful order. 29, 51, 73, 95, 117, 139

WR-E-1.C.0.3 Guides the reader through the piece with transitions and transitional elements. 36, 48, 51, 95, 114, 117, 139, 150

WR-E-1.C.0.4 Provides effective closure. 36, 48, 51, 114, 117, 139, 150

TOPIC: Sentences WR-E-1.D
Creates effective sentences.

WR-E-1.D.0.1 Varies structure and length of sentences. 27, 29, 40, 41, 45, 49, 51, 55, 62, 63, 70, 77, 81, 93, 95, 114, 117, 121, 129, 133, 139, 149, 151, 153

WR-E-1.D.0.2 Writes complete and correct sentences. 10, 11, 18, 19, 22, 23, 26, 27, 29, 32, 36, 37, 40, 41, 44, 45, 47, 48, 49, 51, 55, 62, 63, 66, 70, 72, 77, 80, 81, 84, 88, 92, 93, 95, 98, 99, 101, 102, 114, 117, 120, 121, 127, 128, 129, 131, 133, 136, 137, 139, 148, 149, 150, 151, 152, 153, 155

TOPIC: Language WR-E-1.E
Demonstrates appropriate word choice and grammar.

WR-E-1.E.0.1 Uses effective word choice. 29, 73, 117, 139

WR-E-1.E.0.2 Chooses strong verbs and nouns. 117, 139

WR-E-1.E.0.3 Includes concrete and/or sensory details. 139

WR-E-1.E.0.4 Uses language appropriate to the content, purpose, and audience. 139

WR-E-1.E.0.6 Uses correct usage/grammar. 10, 11, 14, 18, 19, 22, 23, 26, 27, 29, 32, 33, 36, 37, 40, 44, 45, 49, 51, 54, 58, 59, 62, 63, 65, 66, 67, 70, 71, 73, 76, 77, 80, 81, 84, 88, 89, 93, 98, 99, 102, 103, 106, 107, 110, 111, 114, 120, 121, 124, 125, 128, 129, 133, 136, 137, 149, 150, 151, 152, 153, 154, 155

TOPIC: Correctness WR-E-1.F
Demonstrates attention to editing and proofreading.

WR-E-1.F.0.1 Uses correct spelling. 11, 15, 22, 23, 26, 29, 33, 37, 48, 51, 58, 59, 62, 66, 71, 73, 80, 85, 88, 89, 95, 99, 106, 110, 117, 124, 125, 128, 129, 132, 133, 137, 139, 150, 152, 153, 154, 155

WR-E-1.F.0.2 Uses correct punctuation. 10, 11, 14, 15, 18, 22, 27, 29, 36, 41, 44, 45, 48, 49, 51, 55, 62, 63, 66, 73, 80, 51, 84, 85, 88, 89, 92, 95, 99, 102, 111, 114, 120, 121, 124, 125, 128, 129, 133, 136, 139, 148, 149, 152, 153, 154

WR-E-1.F.0.3 Uses correct capitalization. 10, 11, 14, 23, 26, 29, 32, 33, 40, 41, 48, 49, 51, 54, 55, 63, 67, 70, 71, 73, 76, 77, 80, 81, 85, 92, 93, 95, 102, 103, 120, 121, 128, 132, 133, 136, 137, 139, 149, 153. 154, 155

STRAND: Personal Writing WR-E-1.2

TOPIC: Focuses on life experiences using the form personal narrative (focusing on the significance of a single event) or memoir (focusing on the significance of the relationship of the writer with a particular person, place, animal, or thing).

WR-E-1.2.0.1 Develops ideas based on personal experience. 28–29

WR-E-1.2.0.2 Includes sensory details. 29

WR-E-1.2.0.3 Focuses on writer's thoughts and feelings. 116–117

WR-E-1.2.0.4 Writes in first person point-of-view. 29, 116–117

WR-E-1.2.0.5 Includes dialogue where appropriate. 95

STRAND: Literary Writing WR-E-1.3

TOPIC: Communicates about the human condition using literary forms such as poems, short stories, and scripts.

WR-E-1.3.0.1 Uses literary elements of the selected form (e.g., short story—character; poem—rhythm; script—stage directions). 94–95, 117, 139

WR-E-1.3.0.2 Incorporates descriptive language. 69, 75, 95, 139

WR-E-1.3.0.4 Effectively orders events, impressions, and descriptions. 139

TOPIC: Using a variety of forms informs or persuades audiences by presenting ideas and information to accomplish realistic purposes like those students will encounter in their lives.

WR-E-1.4.0.1 Writes letters. 124

WR-E-1.4.0.9 Presents information to engage the reader and to clarify and justify purposes. 50–51

WR-E-1.4.0.10 Communicates the specific purpose for an intended audience. 50–51

WR-E-1.4.0.11 Provides explanation and support to help the reader understand purpose. 50–51, 101, 127, 131

WR-E-1.4.0.12 Supports well-organized idea (e.g., facts, examples, reasons, comparisons, anecdotes, descriptive detail, charts, diagrams, photos/pictures) to accomplish the specific purpose. 50–51

WR-E-1.4.0.13 Includes effective conclusions. 50–51

Notes

Notes

Kentucky
Core Content
Test Preparation
for Reading

Grade 3

Orlando   Austin   Chicago   New York   Toronto   London   San Diego

Visit *The Learning Site!*
www.harcourtschool.com

CONTENTS

Tips for Taking a Test

Preparation Pays Off

It is important to be prepared and to pay attention to the teacher when you take a test. Think about how you can be ready for a test. Then read the tips below.

Tips for Listening

1. Sit quietly.
2. Look at the speaker.
3. Listen for directions.
4. Ignore distractions.

Tips for Writing

1. Sit straight and comfortably in your chair.
2. Have sharpened pencils ready.
3. Keep your eyes on the test booklet.

Mark It Correctly

Answer choices must be marked carefully when you take a test.

DIRECTIONS

Follow the directions for each item below.

Answer Sheet

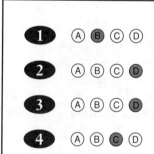

1. Mark answer choice B.
2. Mark answer choice D.
3. What letter follows C here?
4. What letter comes before D here?

Signs Along the Way

Look at the words in the boxes below. Think about what you should do when you see these words on a test. Then answer the questions.

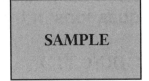

1 Which sign tells you how to do a test section?

    Ⓐ GO ON

    Ⓑ DIRECTIONS

    Ⓒ STOP

    Ⓓ SAMPLE

3 Which sign tells you to put your pencil down?

    Ⓐ GO ON

    Ⓑ DIRECTIONS

    Ⓒ STOP

    Ⓓ SAMPLE

2 Which sign tells you to continue working?

    Ⓐ GO ON

    Ⓑ DIRECTIONS

    Ⓒ STOP

    Ⓓ SAMPLE

4 Which sign tells you that you will read an example of a question?

    Ⓐ GO ON

    Ⓑ DIRECTIONS

    Ⓒ STOP

    Ⓓ SAMPLE

**Don't STOP.
GO ON!**

Following Directions

When you begin a test section, read the directions carefully. Pay attention to words in special type.

Read the information in the left column below. Then answer the questions in the right column.

DIRECTIONS

What is the *main* reason this story was written?

1 What is the important word from this question?

Ⓐ written

Ⓑ main

Ⓒ story

Ⓓ reason

• •

DIRECTIONS

Read the passage. Then read each question about the passage. Decide which is the best answer.

Something that is <u>perplexing</u> is —

2 What should you do after you read the passage?

Ⓐ Answer the most difficult question.

Ⓑ Reread the passage.

Ⓒ Read the question.

Ⓓ Finish the last section.

3 What is the important word from this question?

Ⓐ Something

Ⓑ that

Ⓒ perplexing

Ⓓ is

© Harcourt

Read the Questions

After you read a question, ask yourself, "What is this question really asking?"

Read the questions in the left column. Think about what they are asking. Then answer the questions in the right column.

Michael went in the house to —

Ⓐ feed the dogs

Ⓑ watch TV

Ⓒ answer the phone

Ⓓ finish his homework

1 **What is this question really asking?**

Ⓐ What is the author's purpose?

Ⓑ What did a character do?

Ⓒ What is a character's opinion?

Ⓓ both A and B

• •

Another good title for this story is —

Ⓐ "Baseball Greats"

Ⓑ "Women's Basketball"

Ⓒ "Playing the Court"

Ⓓ "Dribble, Pass, and Shoot"

2 **What is this question really asking?**

Ⓐ What is the main idea?

Ⓑ What happens first?

Ⓒ Who is the main character?

Ⓓ What is the point of view?

Directions

Read this story about a visit to a police station. Then answer Questions 1 through 4. You may look back at the story.

Lost and Found

"Why do we have to go to the police station?" Jimmy asked. He was a little nervous. Only police officers and bad guys went to police stations. Jimmy knew that from TV.

"Remember the backpack we found in the park?" his dad asked. "Well, we need to tell the police about it."

> **Tip**
> When you come to a long word you don't know, first look to see if it is a compound word. Then see if you can read the smaller parts.

"Why can't we keep it?" Jimmy said. "It's just a backpack." He wondered why they were going to all this trouble for one backpack. There were so many other things they could do today.

"What if you lost your backpack?" Dad said. "You would want someone to turn it in, right?" Jimmy thought about that while his dad parked the car.

Jimmy held his dad's hand as they went into the police station. A woman was sitting at a desk. She wore a police uniform, but she didn't look scary. As a matter of fact, she looked very nice.

"How can I help you?" she asked Jimmy's dad. She listened as Jimmy's dad told her about the backpack.

Meanwhile, Jimmy looked around the station. There were no bad guys in handcuffs! This was just a clean, quiet room with booklets and flyers. It didn't seem scary at all.

> **Tip**
> In this paragraph, the author describes Jimmy's new feelings about the police station. This paragraph helps explain the main idea in the passage.

Jimmy looked at the booklets. There were some that told about neighborhood-watch workshops or tips on keeping your house safe. Some had information about when to call 911 for help. There was even a flyer about a summer program for the children in town.

"Come on, Jimmy," his dad called, holding the door. "We're all done. The police will take it from here."

Jimmy took one of the flyers. Maybe he'd try a program this summer, he thought. The activities sounded fun and interesting. Besides, it would be fun to come back to the police station.

1 **What is the story mostly about?**

○ Jimmy finds some interesting things in a backpack.

● Jimmy visits a police station and finds that it is not scary.

○ Jimmy watches a police show on TV.

○ Jimmy signs up for a summer program.

2 **Which word from the story is a compound word?**

● handcuffs

○ handy

○ flyer

○ uniform

3 **Which event from the story happens last?**

○ Jimmy's dad talks to the officer.

○ Jimmy and his dad walk into the station.

● Jimmy takes a flyer about a summer program.

○ Jimmy asks why he can't keep the backpack.

> **Tip**
> As you read each choice, think about where it occurred in the passage. Choose the event that happened last.

4 **What were two things Jimmy read about in the booklets at the police station?**

Answers will vary. Possible answers: Jimmy read

about neighborhood-watch workshops. Jimmy read

about when to call 911 for help. Jimmy read about

tips for keeping your house safe. Jimmy read about

summer programs for children.

> **Tip**
> Reread the paragraph where Jimmy looks at the booklets. Find two possible topics to use for your answers.

Directions

For Questions 5 through 7, read the story and look at the numbered, underlined parts. Choose the answer choices with the correct capital letters, punctuation, and grammar. If the underlined part is correct, mark "Correct."

Boswick is my cat . He sleeping on my bed every night. He plays with
       (5)   (6)

paper. he is a good friend.
       (7)

5 ○ boswick is my cat.
○ Boswick is My cat.
○ Boswick is my Cat.
● Correct

Tip
Remember that only proper nouns begin with a capital letter.

6 ● He sleeps
○ He will sleeping
○ He is sleeps
○ Correct

7 ○ paper? he
● paper. He
○ paper he
○ paper, he

8 Read the sentence and choose the correct punctuation mark.

How many coins do you have

● ?   ○ .   ○ !   ○ ,

Tip
Read the sentence to yourself. Is it asking a question, making a statement, showing strong emotion, or making a pause?

© Harcourt

Directions

Look at the sentence in the box. The sentence has two mistakes in capital letters, punctuation, or grammar. Find the two mistakes and correct them. Mark through each mistake or use editing marks. If needed, write the correction above the mistake.

9

Bobby and i fished at the lake on Tuesday

I.,.

Directions Choose the word that is spelled correctly.

10 The children watched the _____ perform tricks.

- ● puppy
- ○ puppie
- ○ pupy
- ○ pupie

Directions Which sentence below is in an order that makes sense?

11 ○ A Brian has backpack.

○ Are books in six the backpacks.

○ To return me the books.

● The backpack hangs from a hook.

> **Tip**
> Read each choice carefully. Choose the answer that makes sense.

© Harcourt

STOP

Directions

Read this story about a birthday celebration. Then answer Questions 1 through 4. You may look back at the story.

Happy Birthday, Miguel

It was Miguel's birthday, and he and his parents were eating dinner at Pato's, Miguel's favorite restaurant. The food was delicious, but Miguel liked Pato's mariachi band even more than the food.

Mariachis are singers who play and sing traditional Mexican songs. Miguel watched as the mariachis walked from table to table and sang for the customers. People always clapped. "I wish I could be a mariachi," Miguel thought.

Just then, the band moved toward Miguel's table. One of the mariachis smiled at Miguel. "You look very happy this evening," he said.

"It's my birthday," Miguel replied.

"Really? Then may we sing the Birthday Song in Spanish for you?"

Miguel thought for a moment. "I would love that," he said. "But there is something I would like even more."

Miguel whispered to the mariachi. "I think we can do that," the mariachi said, and he put his hat on Miguel. Then he said, "Everyone, this is Miguel. It is his birthday, so he is going to help us sing the Birthday Song!"

When they were finished, everyone clapped and cheered. It was Miguel's best birthday ever.

Tip
The first paragraph introduces the main character and the setting.

Tip
When you come to a word that you don't know, such as a word from a different language, read the words before or after it to figure out what the unknown word means.

1 **Who is the main character in this story?**

    ○ Pato

    ● Miguel

    ○ Mariachi

    ○ The parents

2 **What is a <u>mariachi</u>?**

    ○ a person who cooks delicious food

    ● a person who plays and sings Mexican songs

    ○ a person celebrating a birthday

    ○ a person who claps and cheers loudly

3 **Here are some events from the story. Place the events in order from 1 to 4 by writing the numbers in the boxes next to each sentence.**

    [3] Miguel sings with the band.

    [4] Everyone claps and cheers.

    [2] Miguel says, "It's my birthday."

    [1] Miguel and his parents go to Pato's.

> **Tip**
> Find each choice again by rereading the story. Then number the choices as they appear in the story.

4 **Why do Miguel's parents take him to the restaurant?**

    ○ They are running errands at suppertime.

    ○ Miguel has won a writing contest.

    ● They are celebrating Miguel's birthday.

    ○ Miguel and his parents are on vacation.

Directions

For Questions 5 through 7, read the story and look at the numbered, underlined parts. Choose the answer choices with the correct capital letters, punctuation, and grammar. If the underlined part is correct, mark "Correct."

Terry are a good baseball player. She can hit the ball far? She can easily
(5)   (6)

catch pop flies or Ground balls.
                   (7)

5 ◯ Terry am a

◯ Terry were a

⬤ Terry is a

◯ Correct

6 ◯ Far. She

⬤ far. She

◯ far, She

◯ Correct

7 ◯ Or ground balls.

⬤ or ground balls.

◯ or Ground Balls.

◯ Correct

Tip

Think about the kinds of words that should be capitalized. Are any of these words proper nouns or at the beginning of a sentence?

8 Read the sentence and choose the correct punctuation mark.

That is the biggest strawberry I have ever seen

◯ ?

◯ .

◯ "

⬤ !

Tip

As you read the sentence, think about what kind of emotion you should use. This can help you decide on the correct punctuation.

© Harcourt

*D*irections

Look at the sentence in the box. The sentence has two mistakes in capital letters, punctuation, or grammar. Find the two mistakes and correct them. Mark through each mistake or use editing marks. If needed, write the correction above the mistake.

9 | Please pass sarah a piece of paper? |

Sarah, .

Directions Choose the word that is spelled correctly and completes the sentence.

10 The frog jumped into the _____.

- ○ pound
- ○ ponned
- ● pond
- ○ pont

> **Tip**
> Read the sentence with the words in place. Say the word softly to yourself. What letters make the sounds you hear?

Directions Which sentence below is punctuated correctly?

11 ● How many dimes are in your pocket?

○ How many dimes, are in your pocket.

○ How many dimes are in your pocket.

○ How many dimes are in your pocket!

> **Tip**
> Read each sentence carefully, pausing at commas and using the proper emotion for each punctuation mark.

© Harcourt

STOP

Directions
Read this story about a surprise on a hike. Then answer Questions 1 through 4. You may look back at the story.

The Rabbit Hat

Amy and her older sister, Ellen, always had fun together. Amy thought Ellen knew about a lot of things, especially nature. The sisters had made plans for a hike in the woods on Saturday.

When Saturday arrived, Amy and Ellen got up early and packed their lunches and cameras. They hoped to take some pictures of plants and animals.

As they walked down the path in the woods, Ellen suddenly stopped and stood very still. "Look," she said quietly. She pointed to a spot on the path ahead of them. "Get your camera quickly."

> **Tip**
> As you read, try to predict what will happen next. What do you think Ellen sees?

Amy stared ahead. Through the shadows made by the trees, she saw something round and white sitting on the path.

"It's a rabbit," Amy whispered. "It's sitting so quietly!" Amy snapped five pictures of the rabbit. The girls watched the rabbit for a little while. The animal did not move. Maybe it was hurt.

"Maybe it has a broken leg," Amy said. "What should we do?"

"Let's get a better look," said Ellen.

Amy crept closer. She got close enough to look carefully at the round, white thing. She looked for the cottontail and rabbit ears. She didn't see them. Ellen looked at the white thing, too. Then she picked it up.

> **Tip**
> When decoding a long word, first look to see if it is a compound word. Then break the word into syllables.

"It looks like a rabbit," Ellen exclaimed, "but it's only a baseball cap! Now you'll have five pictures of it!"

Amy and Ellen began to laugh. They laughed so hard that they had to sit down.

1 **What is this story mostly about?**

⬤ a walk in the woods

◯ a day at the seashore

◯ Amy's new pet

◯ how to use a camera

2 **Why do Amy and Ellen stand still?**

◯ They are tired, and they want to rest.

⬤ They think they see a rabbit and do not want to scare it.

◯ They are trying to decide which path to take.

◯ Amy thought she had dropped her camera.

3 **Which word below rhymes with the first syllable of carefully?**

◯ bar

⬤ hair

◯ sort

◯ harp

Tip

First divide *carefully* into syllables. Say only the first syllable as you read the word choices, looking for the one that rhymes.

4 **How do you think Amy and Ellen feel after Ellen picks up the white thing?**

Answers will vary. Possible answer: Amy and Ellen

probably felt surprised and a little embarrassed about

their mistake.

_____

Tip

To help you decide how the girls feel, look for examples of what they say and do in the story.

Name _____

Directions

For Questions 5 through 7, read the story and look at the numbered, underlined parts. Choose the answer choices with the correct capital letters, punctuation, and grammar. If the underlined part is correct, mark "Correct."

Ants live <u>together. In colonies.</u> Each <u>ant have</u> a special job. They work
                    (5)   (6)

together <u>to survive?</u>
          (7)

5 ◯ together. in colonies
  ◯ together? in colonies
  ⬤ together in colonies
  ◯ Correct

6 ⬤ ant has
  ◯ ants has
  ◯ ant is
  ◯ Correct

Tip
The verb needs to match the noun. Read the words carefully and listen for the noun and verb that sound correct.

7 ◯ to survived.
  ⬤ to survive.
  ◯ to surviving.
  ◯ Correct

8 Read the sentence and choose the correct punctuation mark.

Bees live in a hive

   ?   !   .   '
  ◯   ◯   ⬤   ◯

© Harcourt

*D*irections

Look at the sentence in the box. The sentence has two mistakes in capital letters, punctuation, or grammar. Find the two mistakes and correct them. Mark through each mistake or use editing marks. If needed, write the correction above the mistake.

9 | Duncan found a book saturday and returns it to the library.

Saturday, returned

10 What type of sentence is the one below?

Please give me that piece of paper.

○ statement

○ question

● command

○ exclamation

Tip
This kind of sentence makes a request.

Directions Choose the answer that makes a complete sentence.

11 _____ sat together in the back of the bus.

● Several girls

○ One of those

○ Into the forest

○ Looked out

Tip
Read the sentence four times, placing each choice in the blank. Choose the answer that makes the sentence a complete thought.

© Harcourt

STOP

Directions

Read this story about a visit to a music store. Then answer Questions 1 through 4. You may look back at the story.

Emil Plays the Piano

Every day on the way to the bus stop, Emil passed the music store. Through the window he could see a big, black, shiny piano. It looked so pretty that Emil wanted to touch it.

One day the bus came too early. Even though they ran, Emil and his mother could not catch it.

"Now what are we going to do?" asked his mother. "There isn't another bus for half an hour."

"Let's go into the music store," Emil said.

"Why do you want to go in there?" his mother asked, but she let Emil guide her inside.

In the store, Emil walked quickly to the piano. His mother told him not to touch it. Then a man came from behind the counter and smiled. "The piano is there so people can play it," he said.

He helped Emil up onto the piano bench. "See?" the man said, playing a few notes.

Emil put his fingers on the same keys the man had pressed. The notes played together made a little tune, which pleased Emil.

The man's eyebrows went up. "That was good," he said. "Do you play music?"

"No," Emil said.

"They have classes at his school," his mother said. "We should see if Emil can take lessons there."

"That's a very good way to start," the man said. He smiled at Emil. "Maybe someday you'll be playing a piano just like this one."

> **Tip**
> As you read, think about each event in the story and how it causes the next event to occur.

> **Tip**
> Pay attention to the actions in the story and the man's words. They give you clues as to what kind of person he is.

1 **Why do Emil and his mother go into the music store?**

  ◯ to get out of the rain

  ◯ to buy a piano

  ⬤ to wait for the next bus

  ◯ to visit a friend

2 **Choose the word from the fifth paragraph that has the same meaning as the word lead.**

  ◯ asked

  ⬤ guide

  ◯ inside

  ◯ why

3 **What can you tell about Emil from this story?**

Answers will vary. Possible answer: Emil has an

interest in piano as well as some natural talent for

playing it.

Tip
Write your answer in complete sentences. Be sure to write about Emil and what he does on the piano.

4 **Which word best describes the man as he hears Emil play?**

  ◯ frightened

  ◯ bored

  ⬤ surprised

  ◯ annoyed

Tip
Think about the actions and the man's words in the story. They can help you decide which word choice best describes the man.

© Harcourt

Directions

For Questions 5 through 7, read the story and look at the numbered, underlined parts. Choose the answer choices with the correct capital letters, punctuation, and grammar. If the underlined part is correct, mark "Correct."

I got <u>two slice</u> of bread. I put peanut butter on <u>one I put</u> jelly on the other.
     (5)   (6)

Then I ate my <u>delicious sandwich</u>
                  (7)

5
- ○ to slices
- ○ two sliced
- ● two slices
- ○ Correct

6
- ● one. I put
- ○ one. I putted
- ○ one? I put
- ○ Correct

7
- ○ delicious Sandwich.
- ○ delicious sandwich?
- ● delicious sandwich!
- ○ Correct

> **Tip**
> To help you make the right choice, read the entire sentence and then look at how each choice is different. Use clue words from the sentence to make your choice.

8 Which word is a noun in the sentence below?

The little boy ran away.

- ○ little
- ● boy
- ○ ran
- ○ away

> **Tip**
> A noun is a person, a place, a thing, or an idea.

© Harcourt

Name _____

Directions

Look at the sentence in the box. The sentence has two mistakes in capital letters, punctuation, or grammar. Find the two mistakes and correct them. Mark through each mistake or use editing marks. If needed, write the correction above the mistake.

9 | The Rogers gone on their vacation on Monday, may 23.

went, May.

Directions Which choice best completes the sentence below?

10 A small black dog _____.

- ● barked loudly all night
- ○ behind the fence
- ○ almost decided to
- ○ really soft fur

Tip
This sentence is missing a predicate. Remember that the predicate tells the action in the sentence.

Directions Choose the word that is spelled correctly.

11 That _____ scored the most points.

- ○ plaier
- ○ playur
- ● player
- ○ plaer

STOP

Name _____

Directions

Read this selection about Jim Thorpe, a famous athlete. Then answer Questions 1 through 4. You may look back at the selection.

Jim Thorpe: Olympian

Jim Thorpe and his twin brother, Charles, were born on May 28, 1887. They were born in a one-room cabin in Oklahoma Territory. They grew up with other Native Americans on the reservation. Jim's Indian name was Wa-Tho-Huk, which means "Bright Path." He started playing football when he was in college for a famous coach named Pop Warner. He became an important athlete for his school and excelled at baseball, football, and track.

Tip

Think about the main idea of a paragraph as you read it. The subtitles can help give you clues about the main idea of each paragraph.

A Gold Medal Winner

The first Olympic Games that Jim played in were in 1912. He won two gold medals! When a newspaper reported that he had played for a semi-professional baseball team in 1909 and 1910, his medals were taken away and his records erased. There used to be a rule that players weren't allowed to play in the Olympics and also play professional sports. His family tried for many years to get the medals back. Finally, in 1983, the Olympic Committee returned the medals to Jim's children.

Tip

Do not try to remember every date. Use dates to understand the sequence of events. You can always look back at the selection if a question asks about a date.

A Valuable Player

In the same year that Jim won two gold medals, he led his college team to the national championship. He scored 25 touchdowns and 198 points in the same game! In one baseball game, Jim hit three home runs into three different states in the same game. He was playing a baseball game on the Texas-Oklahoma-Arkansas border. He hit the first home run over left field into Oklahoma, his second over right field into Arkansas, and his third into centerfield, which was in Texas.

Later Years

In 1920, Jim Thorpe became the first president of the National Football League. Then, in 1950, he was named the most outstanding athlete of the first half of the twentieth Century by the nation's press. In 1963, Jim was elected to the Football Hall of Fame, ten years after he died.

1 Choose the word from the first paragraph that has the opposite meaning of the word <u>failed</u>.

○ reservation

● excelled

○ became

○ coach

2 What is this selection mostly about?

● Jim Thorpe's success as a great athlete

○ how Jim Thorpe helped his family

○ when Jim Thorpe took a vacation

○ why Jim Thorpe liked sports

3 What happened because Jim played semi-professional baseball?

○ He had a bright path ahead of him.

○ He won several gold medals.

○ He was named an outstanding athlete.

● His gold medals were taken away.

Tip

All of the answer choices happened in the selection. Select the choice that happened because he played semi-professional baseball.

4 Jim Thorpe became the president of a sports league. Which picture below represents that sport?

Tip

Jim Thorpe played all of the sports shown in the pictures. Skim the selection to find the sports league for which he served as president.

○　　　　○　　　　○　　　　●

© Harcourt

GO ON

Name _____

Directions

For Questions 5 through 7, read the story and look at the numbered, underlined parts. Choose the answer choices with the correct capital letters and punctuation. If the underlined part is correct, mark "Correct."

The children played hockey <u>on saturday</u>. Tara brought the
(5)

<u>goal nets. And helmets.</u> <u>Thomas carry</u> snacks for everyone.
(6)   (7)

5 ● on Saturday
   ○ under Saturday
   ○ in Saturday
   ○ Correct

6 ○ goal nets. and helmets.
   ○ goal nets. And Helmets.
   ● goal nets and helmets.
   ○ Correct

7 ○ Thomas carrying
   ● Thomas carried
   ○ Thomas was carry
   ○ Correct

> **Tip**
> Think about sentence fragments and complete sentences when you are reading this passage.

8 Choose the word that <u>best</u> completes the sentence.

Six _____ sang a song at the concert.
   ○ sister
   ○ sisteres
   ● sisters
   ○ sister's

Grade 3   26   GO ON

Directions

Look at the sentence in the box. The sentence has two mistakes in capital letters, punctuation, or grammar. Find the two mistakes and correct them. Mark through each mistake or use editing marks. If needed, write the correction above the mistake.

9 | Six students, asked if them could paint. | *delete comma, they*

10 **Which sentence below has a compound subject?**

- ● Maples and poplars make good shade trees.
- ○ This oak tree was planted years ago.
- ○ The people in the town take care of the trees.
- ○ An apple tree provides shade and fruit.

← **Tip**
A compound subject has two or more subjects joined together in one sentence. Remember that a subject tells *who* or *what* did something.

Directions **What is the purpose of the sentence below?**

11 **In the winter, Canadian geese make their home here.**

- ○ ask a question
- ● make a statement
- ○ give a command
- ○ state a strong feeling

© Harcourt

STOP

Directions

WRITE A PERSONAL NARRATIVE   Think about a family event or holiday that you remember well. Write a personal narrative about the experience. Include sensory details that help to describe the event.

Use the story map below to plan your narrative. Then write the narrative on a separate sheet of paper. When you are finished with the draft, use the Writing Checklist to revise and edit your work. Make a final copy of your story, and draw a picture to go with it.

Family Event or Holiday:

When and where did this event take place?	**Who attended this event?**

How did the event begin?

What interesting things happened during the event?

How did the event end?

Writing Checklist

❏ Did I tell about an interesting family event or holiday?

❏ Does my narrative have a clear beginning, middle, and ending?

❏ Did I include details that stick to the topic?

❏ Did my writing use a variety of sentence types and lengths?

❏ Did I use a choice of words that made my writing interesting?

❏ Did I use capital letters and punctuation marks correctly?

❏ Did I spell each word correctly?

STOP

Directions
Read this poem about a day at the beach. Then answer Questions 1 through 4. You may look back at the poem.

Sea Treasures

A feather floating to the ground,

A smooth and foggy bit of glass,

A creature's home that circles round,

Footsteps falling with a splash,

A star that once shown in the sea,

Bring these treasures home to me.

Tip
In this poem, the author uses figurative language, words used outside of their everyday meaning, to help you picture a beach scene.

Tip
What are the treasures mentioned in the poem? Reread each line and think about each "beach treasure" the author is describing.

GO ON

© Harcourt

1 **What is one reason that the author might have written this poem?**

⬤ to describe his or her feelings about the beach

◯ to inform the reader about seagulls at the beach

◯ to persuade the reader to plan a vacation

◯ to make the reader notice the stars in the sky

Directions **Read this sentence from the poem.**

> A star that once shown in the sea.

2 **What does this sentence mean?**

⬤ The author saw a starfish that was once in the water.

◯ The author saw a star from the sky reflecting in the water.

◯ The author saw a star sticker on a piece of paper.

◯ The author saw a kite shaped like a star.

3 **Which of the following words are homophones?**

◯ ground and round

⬤ sea and see

◯ falling and floating

◯ smooth and rough

> **Tip**
> Remember that homophones are words that sound the same, but have different meanings and spellings.

4 **Which picture below is not something described in the poem?**

◯   ◯   ◯   ⬤

> **Tip**
> Because the poem does not specifically name these objects, reread each line carefully. Rule out the objects that are described in the poem.

Directions

For Questions 5 through 7, read the story and look for the numbered, underlined parts. Choose the answer choices with the correct capital letters, punctuation, and grammar. If the underlined part is correct, mark "Correct."

Three lions rested under a tree. The shade provided welcome relief. From the
(5)   (6)

hot sun. The color of their fur helped them blending into the surrounding grasses.
(7)

5 ○ three lions

   ○ Three lion

   ○ Three lion's

   ● Correct

6 ● relief from the

   ○ relief. from the

   ○ relief from. The

   ○ Correct

7 ○ helped them blended

   ● helped them blend

   ○ helped them blends

   ○ Correct

8 Read the sentence and choose the missing punctuation mark.

   I have a pencil an eraser, and a piece of paper.

   ○ !

   ○ ?

   ○ .

   ● ,

> **Tip**
> Look for proper punctuation when proofreading. Also, be sure that a singular or plural noun agrees with the describing word.

© Harcourt

Directions

Look at the sentence in the box. The sentence has two mistakes in capital letters, punctuation, or grammar. Find the two mistakes and correct them. Mark through each mistake or use editing marks. If needed, write the correction above the mistake.

9 | Last tuesday, the weather were rainy and cold. |

Tuesday, was

Directions Choose the word that best completes the sentence.

10 This new pencil is _____ than my pencil.

- ○ longest
- ● longer
- ○ more long
- ○ more longer

Directions Choose the word that is a verb in the sentence below.

11 A green lizard flicked its tongue at the fly.

- ○ green
- ● flicked
- ○ tongue
- ○ at

Tip
Remember that a verb is a word that shows action in a sentence.

© Harcourt

STOP

Directions

Read this selection about the Pony Express. Then answer Questions 1 through 4. You may look back at the selection.

The Pony Express

Before there were planes or even railroads, people invented another way to get mail quickly from place to place. The Pony Express began carrying mail on April 3, 1860, and stopped the service on October 24, 1861.

Tip
As you read, pay attention to the describing words. They will help you understand the details in the selection.

How the Riders Traveled

In the Pony Express, riders took turns carrying the mail by horseback. After about ten miles, riders would change horses. People stood by with fresh horses that were ready to go.

Pony Express riders had to be fast. They wore tight-fitting clothes so the wind wouldn't slow them down. Even the horses were dressed for speed. The saddles used by riders were very thin.

Ready for Speed

The Pony Express lasted only a brief time, but in spite of its short life, it remains a most exciting and interesting piece of American history.

1 **What is this selection mostly about?**

○ The Pony Express has been around for a long time.

● Pony Express riders carried mail by horseback.

○ Horses need light and thin saddles.

○ Pony Express riders changed horses every ten miles or so.

2 **Which word below has the same meaning as <u>brief</u>?**

● short

○ fast

○ smooth

○ long

Tip
Find where the word *brief* is used in the selection. Use the words that come before and after the word to help you determine another word that means the same thing.

3 **Which sentence from the story tells about a cause and an effect?**

○ After about ten miles, riders would change horses.

○ People stood by with fresh horses that were ready to go.

● They wore tight-fitting clothes so the wind wouldn't slow them down.

○ The saddles used by riders were very thin.

4 **According to the selection, what are two ways Pony Express riders made themselves faster?**

Answers will vary. Possible answers: Riders wore

tight-fitting clothes. Riders changed horses often.

Riders' saddles were thin.

Tip
Find details in the selection that tell about how the riders had to be fast. Use complete sentences as you write your answers.

© Harcourt

*D*irections

For Questions 5 and 6, read the story and look at the numbered, underlined parts. Choose the answer choices with the correct capital letters, grammar, and punctuation. If the underlined part is correct, mark "Correct."

Starfish is interesting sea creatures. They have no front end They have arms
  (5)   (6)

that they use to walk. Any arm can lead the way. _____
                                                      (7)

5 ○ Starfishes is

   ● Starfish are

   ○ Starfish am

   ○ Correct

6 ● end. They

   ○ end, they

   ○ end? They

   ○ Correct

7 Choose the sentence that best completes the story above.

   ● Now that is a unique animal!

   ○ I collect starfish on my vacation.

   ○ Many animals live at the beach.

   ○ Clams have two shells.

> **Tip**
>
> Look for a sentence choice that closes the story. Your choice should have the same basic idea as the topic sentence.

© Harcourt

8 Which meaning of <u>close</u> is used in the sentence below?

Patricia lives close to the park.

- ● near
- ○ similar
- ○ shut
- ○ far

Directions Choose the word that is spelled correctly.

9 The boy needed _____ paper.

- ○ moore
- ○ mour
- ● more
- ○ moar

Directions Choose the word that correctly completes the sentence.

10 Mr. Cheswick wrote a book, and _____ donated it to the library.

- ● he
- ○ them
- ○ she
- ○ me

Tip
Try reading each choice in the sentence. Listen for the one that makes sense and sounds correct.

11 Which one is not a complete sentence?

- ○ The students asked the teacher for help.
- ● Four girls and two boys.
- ○ The report was due Friday.
- ○ They studied hard.

Tip
Remember that a complete sentence needs both a subject and a predicate.

STOP

Directions

Read this selection about the wildlife parks in Africa. Then answer Questions 1 through 4. You may look back at the selection.

Wildlife Parks

Hunters are a problem for many wild animals in Africa. These hunters kill too many animals, causing some to disappear completely. In order to protect these animals, many African countries have created huge national parks. The parks serve as safe places for wildlife, and they cover thousands of square miles. People can go to the parks and watch the animals, but they may not harm them.

The Selous Game Reserve

The largest game reserve in the world is located in the African country of Tanzania. The Selous Game Reserve is larger than some countries! Animals that live there include elephants, buffalo, hippos, wild dogs, lions, bushbucks, impalas, giraffes, elands, baboons, zebras, rhinos, kudus, and many types of birds.

Tip

If you come across a long word that begins with a capital letter, and the word is in the middle of a sentence, the word probably names a place, a person, or a thing.

The Serengeti National Park

The second largest park in Tanzania is Serengeti National Park. The name Serengeti, taken from the language of the Maasai people, means "endless plains." At certain seasons of the year, wildebeests and other animals travel across the plains to search for food and water. More than one million wildebeests make this journey, along with huge numbers of zebras and Thomson's gazelles. Lions often follow the wildebeests.

Tip

If a question asks for information about a certain park, you can use the subtitles to quickly locate the section about that park.

In addition to its vast plains, Serengeti National Park also has areas of woodland. Giraffes, which eat leaves from trees, are not found on the plains but do live in other areas of the park. Leopards, flamingos, crocodiles, black rhinos, and cheetahs are other animals that make their homes in the safety of Serengeti National Park.

A Safe Place for Wildlife

Africa has many other parks and reserves. Some African governments have realized that they need to protect the interesting and unusual animals that are found on their continent only. By creating these protected areas, Africa can make sure that the animals will be here in the future.

© Harcourt

1 **Why do you think the author wrote this selection?**

○ to give information about wildebeests

○ to persuade you to take a trip to Africa

○ to entertain readers with funny animal stories

● to give information about wildlife parks in Africa

2 **Why were the wildlife parks created?**

● to make a safe place for animals

○ to use land that was going to waste

○ to make a good place for hunters

○ to grow food for people

3 **Which meaning of** <u>reserve</u> **is used in the selection?**

○ to save someone a seat

● land set aside for a special purpose

○ quiet and shy

○ to give to someone again

4 **According to the selection, which picture below is** <u>not</u> **an animal found in the Serengeti National Park?**

○　　　　○　　　　○　　　　●

Directions

For Questions 5 through 7, read the story and look for the numbered, underlined parts. Choose the answer choices with the correct capital letters, punctuation, and grammar. If the underlined part is correct, mark "Correct."

Alexander waited excitedly for the <u>party to begins</u>. All of <u>his Friends</u> were
                                    (5)   (6)

coming. <u>There would be great snacks. There would be fun games to play.</u>
                                    (7)

It would be a fun day.

5 ○ party to began
   ● party to begin
   ○ party to beginning
   ○ Correct

6 ● his friends
   ○ her Friends
   ○ his friend
   ○ Correct

7 ○ There would be great snacks and also would be fun games.
   ○ There would be great snacks, but fun games to play.
   ● There would be great snacks and fun games to play.
   ○ There would be great snacks to play.

Tip
When combining sentences, look out for words that repeat in both sentences. Only use these words one time.

8 **Which word best completes the sentence below?**

   Yesterday, three puppies ____ in the tall grass.

   ○ rolls   ○ rolling   ○ roll   ● rolled

Tip
Look at the first word in the sentence to decide when the action in the sentence takes place.

© Harcourt

Directions

Look at the sentence in the box. The sentence has two mistakes in capital letters, punctuation, or grammar. Find the two mistakes and correct them. Mark through each mistake or use editing marks. If needed, write the correction above the mistake.

9

Susan and i will ride, the bus to the game.

I, delete comma

10 **Which sentence is punctuated correctly?**

- ⦿ Anna ran fast, but Miko was the winner.
- ◯ Anna ran fast but, Miko was the winner.
- ◯ Anna ran fast, but, Miko was the winner.
- ◯ Anna ran, fast but Miko was the winner.

11 **Write a compound sentence about your school. Capitalize and punctuate it correctly.**

Answers will vary. Possible answer: My school is an

old brick building, but it is a fun place to learn.

_____

_____

Tip

As you read each sentence, remember to pause at each comma. This may help you decide the best place for a comma in the sentence.

Tip

A compound sentence joins together two complete sentences. Use a comma and *and* or *but* to join the two sentences together.

STOP

Directions

Read this story about a little songbird. Then answer Questions 1 through 4. You may look back at the story.

Changing His Tune

Once there was a little bird named George. He sang all day long. Sometimes he'd hear other birds and their songs. George wanted to sing just like them.

As a mockingbird, he was able to imitate other birds.

One day, he was outside singing when his friend Donna flew by. "I'm surprised to see you here, George," she said. "You don't sound like yourself. I thought it was someone else singing."

"I'm singing like Ricky," he said. "Then I plan to sing like Betty and Marco."

"Why don't you sing like yourself?" she asked.

"I like their voices," George said. "I think they sound better than mine."

"That's too bad," Donna replied. "I always thought yours was the best."

When George heard that, he decided to change his tune. From that day on, whenever George sang, he did so in his own voice.

> **Tip**
> Sometimes the title can give you clues about the story. Read the title, and predict what you think the story will be about. Then check your prediction as you read.

> **Tip**
> Quotation marks let you know that someone is talking. The words inside the quotations marks are the exact words that someone is saying.

© Harcourt

GO ON

1 **What would be another good title for this story?**

○ Donna Goes Away

○ Over the Treetops

○ Ricky's Surprise

◉ His Own Voice

2 **How are the words <u>hear</u> and <u>here</u> related?**

○ They are synonyms.

○ They are antonyms.

◉ They are homophones.

○ They are multiple-meaning words.

> **Tip**
> Look carefully at the words. They sound the same, but have different spellings and meanings. What kinds of words are they?

3 **Why is Donna surprised to see George?**

○ She thinks he has moved.

◉ She thinks someone else is singing.

○ She thinks she is alone.

○ She doesn't think George knows how to sing.

4 **How does George change at the end of the story?**

Answers will vary. Possible answers: George decides

that he likes his voice after all and he doesn't need to

copy other birds. He sings with his own voice.

> **Tip**
> Think about George at the beginning of the story. How is George different at the end of the story? Describe both how and why he has changed. Use evidence from the story.

Directions

For Questions 5 through 7, read the story and look for the numbered, underlined parts. Choose the answer choices with the correct capital letters, punctuation, and grammar. If the underlined part is correct, mark "Correct."

Sunflowers are <u>easy to growed</u>. One sunflower plant grows from a little seed.
             (5)

They grow <u>very larger</u> in one season. All they need is <u>some water good soil,</u>
       (6)   (7)

and lots of sunshine.

5 ○ easy to grown

    ○ easily to grow

    ● easy to grow

    ○ Correct

6 ○ very largest

    ● very large

    ○ much largest

    ○ Correct

7 ● some water, good soil

    ○ some water Good soil

    ○ some water. Good soil

    ○ Correct

> **Tip**
> What punctuation mark is used to separate a list of three or more items?

8 Read the sentence and choose the correct punctuation mark.

    Seagulls flew in lazy circles overhead

    ○ ?

    ○ !

    ● .

    ○ "

Directions

Look at the sentence in the box. The sentence has two
mistakes in capital letters, punctuation, or grammar.
Find the two mistakes and correct them. Mark through
each mistake or use editing marks. If needed, write the
correction above the mistake.

9 | I sended a letter to Atlanta Georgia. | sent, Atlanta, Georgia

Directions What kind of sentence is the one below?

Tip
Think about each
answer choice. What
are the features of
each type of sentence?
What are the features
of the example
sentence?

10 The waves looked inviting, but the water was very cold. ◄

○ a simple sentence

● a compound sentence

○ a question

○ an incomplete sentence

11 Which sentence below does not have the
correct punctuation?

Tip
Read each sentence
choice. Use the proper
emotion and voice for
the given punctuation.
Which one needs a
different punctuation
mark?

○ The sky is very cloudy.

○ Do you have your umbrella?

● What happened to my raincoat.

○ Look, there's a rainbow!

STOP

Name _____

D*irections*

Read this selection about the Red Cross. Then answer Questions 1 through 4. You may look back at the selection.

The Red Cross

The American Red Cross began in 1881. Clara Barton, a nurse who cared for soldiers during the Civil War, helped set up the Red Cross in the United States. The Red Cross now has groups in countries around the world.

> **Tip**
> As you read, think about the topic sentence for each paragraph. Then, look for details in the paragraph that support the topic sentence.

To the Rescue

The Red Cross helps people during bad storms such as hurricanes. After a bad storm, people often have trouble finding food. They may not have water that is safe to drink. After tornadoes in Texas and Louisiana, the Red Cross found people new places to stay. Red Cross workers brought food and water to people in California after an earthquake.

Be Prepared

The Red Cross teaches people how to prepare for bad storms. In areas where these storms happen, workers visit schools and give out special booklets of information. The booklets teach people about storms and show them how to protect their homes and families.

Safe Swimming for All

Swimming safety is also an important program offered by the Red Cross. In many communities, Red Cross teachers give swimming classes to children as young as four years old. They also teach older people. They have special classes to prepare people to become lifeguards.

> **Tip**
> If you have trouble reading a long word such as *communitites*, try breaking the word into syllables. Then, use words that come before and after to help you figure out the meaning of this long word.

© Harcourt

1 **What is this selection mostly about?**

○ The Red Cross plants many gardens.

● The Red Cross helps people in many ways.

○ The Red Cross sells clothes to people.

○ The Red Cross tells stories.

Tip

Choose the answer that best describes the main idea of the selection.

2 **Which word from the selection is a compound word?**

○ workers

○ swimming

○ information

● lifeguards

3 **Who was Clara Barton?**

○ a woman soldier

○ a teacher

● an American nurse

○ a woman the Red Cross helped after a storm

Tip

If you do not remember details about a person, skim over the selection until you find the person's name. Then reread to find the details you need.

4 **Why do you think the subtitle for paragraph 2 is called "To the Rescue"?**

Answers will vary. Possible answer: The paragraph

talks about how the Red Cross helps people after bad

storms or disasters. They come to the rescue of

people in trouble.

Directions

For Questions 5 and 6, read the story and look for the numbered, underlined parts. Choose the answer choices with the correct capital letters, punctuation, and grammar. If the underlined part is correct, mark "Correct."

Moths have ways to protect themselves. <u>Some Moths</u> have circles like eyes
(5)

to scare off <u>predators? Other</u> moths have colors that tell birds they are poisonous.
(6)

Moths even have camouflage markings that let them hide easily.

5 ● Some moths

○ Some moth

○ some moths

○ Correct

6 ○ predators other

● predators. Other

○ predators, Other

○ Correct

> **Tip**
> Think about how each punctuation mark changes the way you would read the sentence.

7 Choose the sentence that would <u>best</u> complete the story above.

○ Butterflies eat the nectar from flowers.

● Moths may be small, but they know how to stay safe.

○ Insects hatch from eggs.

○ Some animals are only active at night.

8 Choose the word that is spelled correctly and completes the sentence.

> **Tip**
> Slowly say the sounds the letters make before you make your choice.

My parrot is _____ to sing songs.

● trained   ○ traynd   ○ trayed   ○ tranned

© Harcourt

Name _____

*D*irections

Look at the sentence in the box. The sentence has two mistakes in capital letters, punctuation, or grammar. Find the two mistakes and correct them. Mark through each mistake or use editing marks. If needed, write the correction above the mistake.

9 | Mrs. maggie Jones will be my teacher, next year.

Maggie, teacher next

Directions Choose the adjective in the sentence below.

10 A beautiful flower grows through the fence.

- ● beautiful
- ○ flower
- ○ grows
- ○ through

Tip
Remember that an adjective is a word that describes a noun.

Directions Choose the **best** way to combine the sentences below.

11 Sara flew a paper kite. Miles flew a paper kite.

- ○ Sara but Miles flew a paper kite.
- ○ Sara flew a kite and Miles flew a kite.
- ● Sara and Miles flew a paper kite.
- ○ Sara flew a paper kite and so did Miles fly a kite.

Tip
You can combine sentence subjects if two sentences have the same predicate.

© Harcourt

Lesson 10

49

STOP

Name _____

D*irections*

WRITE AN INFORMATIVE PARAGRAPH Imagine that your family has decided to get a new pet. What does it take to keep this pet happy and healthy? How would your family have to work together to take care of this pet? Write a paragraph about how to take care of this pet and what you and your family should do to prepare your home for it.

Use the graphic organizer below to plan your paragraph. Then write the paragraph on a separate sheet of paper. When you are finished with the draft, use the Writing Checklist to revise and edit your work. Make a final copy of your informative paragraph, and draw a picture to go with it.

Type of Pet We Want:

Ideas about Pet Care	Changes My Family Will Need to Make
Food and Water:	
Where It Will Live and Sleep:	
Safety:	
Exercise:	

Conclusion about Caring for our New Pet:

© Harcourt

Grade 3

50

GO ON

Writing Checklist

❏ Does my opening clearly state the type of pet we want?

❏ Did I describe the needs of our new pet in detail?

❏ Did I give examples about how our home needs to change to meet our pet's needs?

❏ Did I end my paragraph with a conclusion about caring for our new pet?

❏ Did I use a variety of simple and compound sentences?

❏ Did I use singular and plural nouns effectively and correctly?

❏ Did I use capital letters and punctuation marks correctly?

❏ Did I spell words correctly?

❏ Did I write neatly?

STOP

Directions

Read this selection about making popcorn. Then answer Questions 1 through 4. You may look back at the selection.

Making Popcorn Together

Elena and Josh wanted to watch a movie and eat a snack.

They looked on the shelves in the kitchen and found a package of microwave popcorn. Elena read the directions out loud.

DIRECTIONS

- **Remove the plastic overwrap.**
- **Unfold the bag. Place it in the center of the microwave oven.**
- **Set the microwave oven to high. Popping time is from two to five minutes, depending on the oven. Listen carefully. Stop the oven when popping slows to one or two seconds between pops.**

Remove the bag from the microwave. BE CAREFUL! IT'S VERY HOT! Open the bag by pulling opposite corners. Keep your hands and face away from the hot steam that will escape.

Tip

Notice that each step in the directions begins with a bullet, or black dot. These dots make each step easier to read and understand.

First, Josh and Elena removed the plastic overwrap. They unfolded the bag and placed it in the center of the microwave oven.

Next, they started the microwave. They listened carefully for the popping sounds. When the popping slowed down, they turned off the microwave and removed the bag. They kept their hands away from the steam as they opened the bag.

Tip

While reading, look for time-order words such as First and Next. They can help you place events in the correct order.

They poured the popcorn into a large bowl. Then they went to watch a movie.

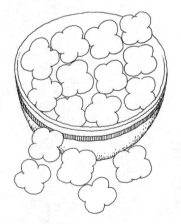

1 What is this selection mostly about?

○ why popcorn pops

○ the history of popcorn

● making popcorn

○ where to buy popcorn

2 At the beginning of the selection, what do Elena and Josh want to do?

○ play a game and watch TV

● watch a movie and eat a snack

○ play outside

○ cook dinner in the microwave

> **Tip**
> The words At the beginning of the story are clues to the answer. Skim the first few sentences of the selection to find the answer.

3 Which word means the opposite of careful?

○ helpful

● thoughtless

○ angry

○ moody

4 Here are some steps from the selection. Place the steps in order from 1 to 4 by writing the numbers in the boxes next to each sentence.

[4] The children pour the popcorn into a bowl.

[1] Josh and Elena place the unfolded bag in the center of the microwave.

[3] When the popping slows, they remove the bag.

[2] They start the microwave.

> **Tip**
> Look for time-order words in the selection to help you find out the correct order of the steps.

© Harcourt

Directions

For Questions 5 through 7, read the story and look for the numbered, underlined parts. Choose the answer choices with the correct capital letters, grammar, or topic sentence. If an underlined part is correct, mark "Correct."

_____ Inside a volcano, the melted rock is called magma. Once the magma
　　(5)

erupting from the volcano, it is called lava. rock is formed when the lava cools.
　　(6)　　　　　　　　　　　　　　　　　　　　　(7)

5 Choose the best topic sentence for the paragraph.

○ Some rocks are made on the sea floor.

○ I have a rock collection.

○ Have you ever been to Hawaii?

● Some rocks are formed from volcanoes.

> **Tip**
> The topic sentence is the main idea of the paragraph. All of the following sentences give details about the topic sentence.

6 ● erupts from

○ erupt from

○ erupt. From

○ Correct

7 ○ lava rock

○ lava, rock

● lava. Rock

○ Correct

8 Which word best completes the sentence below?

My older _____ hair was wet from the rain.

● sister's

○ sisters

○ sister

○ sisterès

> **Tip**
> Think about this question as you look for the correct answer: What is a shorter way to say "the hair of my older sister"?

© Harcourt

Name _____

Directions

Look at the sentence in the box. The sentence has two mistakes in capital letters, punctuation, or grammar. Find the two mistakes and correct them. Mark through each mistake or use editing marks. If needed, write the correction above the mistake.

9 | Please write you're name at the Top of your paper. | your, top

Directions What is the purpose of the sentence below?

10 Please put your jacket in the closet.

○ make a statement

◉ give a command

○ ask a question

○ state a strong feeling

> **Tip**
> The punctuation at the end of a sentence can give you clues about the type of sentence it is.

11 Which sentence below does <u>not</u> have the correct punctuation?

○ Where are the books for class?

○ Sarah's papers fell out of her backpack.

○ She also lost a pencil, a pen, and a ruler.

◉ John helped her pick things up?

Lesson 11   55

STOP

Directions

Read this story about a family's participation in a county fair. Then answer Questions 1 through 4. You may look back at the story.

Blue Ribbon Squash

It seemed that everyone Harriet knew had won a blue ribbon at the county fair. Aunt Mildred's quilts and Father's corn had won last year. Her sister Sandra had won for an original dress, and some classmates at school had started a "Blue Ribbon Winners" club.

"I have to win a blue ribbon this year!" Harriet told her mother.

"Then you'd better decide what to enter," Mother said, "and get started early."

While visiting her grandfather one summer, Harriet had learned to make a golden squash salad that tasted better than anything else she'd ever eaten. She decided to raise her own squash in a sunny spot by a nearby spring. The first morning of the fair she would select the very best squash and make the delicious salad.

The afternoon before the fair was to begin, however, Harriet's mother announced that Grandfather was coming to visit. He intended to enter his golden squash salad in their county fair. Harriet ran to the spring and sat sadly beside her garden. Her squash had grown huge and full by the pure water and glowed like gold in the late sun. She'd never before seen such beautiful squash.

Suddenly Harriet jumped up, shouting, "I know what I'll do! I'll give Grandfather some small squash for his salad, and I'll enter the biggest one at the fair. We're both sure to win blue ribbons!"

Tip
As you read, look for the problem that the main character has to solve. Then as you read the story, look for clues that the problem has been solved.

Tip
To understand the meaning of a word like *suddenly*, think about the meaning of the suffix *-ly* and the root word *sudden*.

© Harcourt

1 Why does Harriet decide to raise her own squash?

- ● so she can make a salad for the county fair
- ○ so her grandfather will have squash to eat
- ○ so her friends will be impressed
- ○ because her mother tells her to do it

2 What does the word <u>sadly</u> mean in this story?

- ○ not sad
- ○ without being sad
- ● in a sad way
- ○ a person who is sad

3 Read this sentence from the story. What does it mean? ◄

> Her squash glowed like gold in the late sun.

- ○ The squash is worth a lot of money after summer.
- ● The squash is a golden yellow color in the bright light.
- ○ The squash glows in the dark.
- ○ The squash is made of metal, but melts in the sun.

Tip

This sentence is an example of a simile. A simile compares one object to another object using the word *like* or *as*. What is the author comparing the squash to?

4 Why is Harriet's solution to her problem a good one? ◄

Answers will vary. Possible answer: Harriet's solution

is a good one because she will have a squash to

enter in the fair and her grandfather will have a

squash for his salad. They both have a chance to win

at the fair.

Tip

Before you answer this question, be sure you understand the problem Harriet faces. Then find her solution and give reasons why you think it is a good one. Use complete sentences in your answer.

Directions

For Questions 5 through 7, read the story and look for the numbered, underlined parts. Choose the answer choices with the correct capital letters, punctuation, and grammar. If the underlined part is correct, mark "Correct."

The stegosaurus <u>was a unique</u> dinosaur. It had <u>two row of bony plates</u> down
                 (5)   (6)

the center of its back. Its tail <u>was cover</u> with large spikes. Despite its size, the
                                  (7)

stegosaurus had a small narrow head.

5
- ○ were a unique
- ○ am a unique
- ○ are a unique
- ● Correct

6
- ○ too rows of bony plates
- ● two rows of bony plates
- ○ two row of bony plate
- ○ Correct

> **Tip**
> Look carefully at the adjectives to help you decide whether the noun *row* should be singular or plural.

7
- ○ were cover
- ○ was covering
- ● was covered
- ○ Correct

8 Which choice below shows the abbreviation for <u>Kentucky</u>?

  ○ Ktcky.   ● KY   ○ Knty.   ○ KN

© Harcourt

Directions

Look at the sentence in the box. The sentence has two mistakes in capital letters, punctuation, or grammar. Find the two mistakes and correct them. Mark through each mistake or use editing marks. If needed, write the correction above the mistake.

9 | Billys saddle are very old and beautiful. | *Billy's, is*

Directions Choose the word that is spelled correctly.

10 He asked for a glass of water _____ he was thirsty.

- ○ beecuz
- ● because
- ○ becuse
- ○ becouse

11 **Which underlined word is an adjective?**

- ○ Several <u>groups</u> of people watched the parade.
- ○ Colorful blankets <u>covered</u> the grass.
- ● The <u>silly</u> clowns made my little brother laugh.
- ○ The sky <u>was</u> clear and sunny that day.

Tip
Remember that an adjective is a describing word. Often, an adjective will be followed by a noun.

STOP

Name _____

Read this e-mail message about playing soccer. Then answer Questions 1 through 4. You may look back at the message.

An E-mail Message

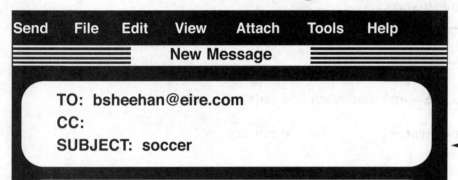

Send   File   Edit   View   Attach   Tools   Help

New Message

TO: bsheehan@eire.com
CC:
SUBJECT: soccer

Tip
The SUBJECT line on an e-mail message tells the receiver what the message is mostly about.

Tip
Look for time-order clues that help you understand the order or sequence of events.

Dear Bridget,

How are you? I am fine. Are you enjoying your summer? I hope you are playing with your friends a lot. I started playing soccer last week, and it's lots of fun. We practice every Monday and Thursday afternoon.

I'm playing goalie, and I made a great catch at practice. The coach was proud.

Our first game is Saturday morning. I'm excited because I think we can win. I will write to tell you how it goes.

I remember you told me that in Ireland soccer is called football. Do you play football? Write back soon.

Your friend,

Mike

1 **Why do you think Mike wrote this message?**

○ to ask Bridget about Ireland

● to tell Bridget that he is playing soccer

○ to persuade Bridget to start swimming

○ to entertain Bridget with some jokes

2 **Which word means the opposite of proud?**

○ silly

○ smooth

● ashamed

○ smiled

> **Tip**
> Remember that you
> want the "opposite" of
> *proud*. Think about
> what *proud* means.
> Then think of words
> that mean the opposite.
> Which choice would
> best match the words
> you thought of?

3 **What is supposed to happen on Saturday morning?**

○ Bridget will have her first football game.

● Mike will have his first soccer game.

○ Mike will go to Ireland.

○ Bridget will go back to school.

4 **Based on this passage, what do you predict Bridget will most likely say in her reply?**

Answers will vary. Possible answer: I predict that

Bridget will tell him that she does play football. She

may also wish Mike good luck in his soccer game.

> **Tip**
> You are asked to
> predict Bridget's
> response. Look for
> evidence in the e-mail
> message that can help
> you make a good
> prediction.

© Harcourt

Name _____

*D*irections

For Questions 5 through 7, read the story and look for the numbered, underlined parts. Choose the answer choices with the correct capital letters, punctuation, and grammar. If the underlined part is correct, mark "Correct."

The gannett is a bird with <u>remarkable feets</u>. Both <u>feet is webbed</u>, like a duck's.
(5)   (6)

The webbed feet are very <u>strong. like swim fins.</u>
(7)

5 ● remarkable feet
   ○ remarkable foot
   ○ remarkable foots
   ○ Correct

Tip
Remember that some plural nouns change their spelling rather than add -s or -es.

6 ○ feet am webbed
   ○ feet was webbed
   ● feet are webbed
   ○ Correct

7 ● strong, like swim fins.
   ○ strong. Like swim fins.
   ○ strong! like swim fins.
   ○ Correct

8 In the sentence below, which pronoun <u>best</u> replaces the underlined words?

You should ask <u>the ball players</u> for their autographs.

   ○ they
   ○ he
   ○ us
   ● them

Tip
Try reading each choice in place of the underlined words in the sentence. Does one choice sound better than the others?

© Harcourt

Directions

Look at the sentence in the box. The sentence has two
mistakes in capital letters, punctuation, or grammar.
Find the two mistakes and correct them. Mark through
each mistake or use editing marks. If needed, write the
correction above the mistake.

9 | Last thursday, we goed to the movies. | Thursday, went

Directions What is the complete predicate in the
sentence below?

10 Jesse and Megan laughed at my jokes.

    ⭕ Jesse, Megan

    ⭕ at my jokes

    ⭕ Megan laughed

    ⬤ laughed at my jokes

> **Tip**
> What is the action in
> this sentence? That will
> help you find the words
> that make up the
> complete predicate.

Directions How should the punctuation be corrected
in the sentence below?

11 Mrs Tyler brought a dessert for the dinner on March 3.

    ⭕ Put a period after <u>March</u>.

    ⭕ Put a comma after <u>March</u>.

    ⬤ Put a period after <u>Mrs</u>.

    ⭕ Put a comma after <u>Tyler</u>.

STOP

Name _____

*D*irections

Read this poem about two brothers. Then answer Questions 1 through 4. You may look back at the poem.

My Brothers

I hear their chatter up the walk,

The thud of the door,

The clunking, thunking, plunking of books and boots,

High-five slaps and laughing whoops.

Enclosed in ordinary joy they have,

They are happy and united.

A noisy twosome of one brotherly love.

> **Tip**
> This poem contains many adjectives that help you picture in your mind the boys' actions and noises.

> **Tip**
> *Unity* and *united* have the same root word—*unit*.

© Harcourt

GO ON

1 **Why did the author probably write this poem?**

○ to inform the reader about books and boots

○ to tell how to behave after school

◉ to entertain the reader with a description of his or her brothers

○ to persuade the reader to go to school

2 **What is the meaning of the word <u>united</u>?**

○ split apart

◉ joined together as one

○ untied like a shoelace

○ quiet

3 **Which of these words <u>best</u> describe the brothers?**

◉ joyful

○ disagreeable

○ unhappy

○ impolite

> **Tip**
> How do most kids feel when they give high-fives?

4 **Read this line from the poem. What do you think it means?**

> The clunking, thunking, plunking of books and boots

Answers will vary. Possible answer: It means that

the boys make a lot of noise when they come home

from school and set things down.

> **Tip**
> In a poem, the words are chosen for their meaning, their sounds, and for the picture they create in a reader's mind.

GO ON

Directions

For Questions 5 through 7, read the story and look for the numbered, underlined parts. Choose the answer choices with the correct capital letters, punctuation, and grammar. If the underlined part is correct, mark "Correct."

Jessica was nervous and excited for the school play <u>to begin. Her</u> classmates
                                                                    (5)

huddled in small <u>whispering groups, backstage</u>. Suddenly, the music started
                              (6)

and Jessica knew it <u>was time to began</u>.
                            (7)

5 ○ to begin her

  ○ to begin? Her

  ○ to began. Her

  ● Correct

6 ● whispering groups backstage

  ○ whisper groups backstage

  ○ whispering groups. Backstage

  ○ Correct

7 ○ was time to begins

  ○ were time to began

  ● was time to begin

  ○ Correct

8 Which word in the sentence below is a possessive noun? ←

The poster's ink was smeared from the rain.

  ● poster's   ○ ink   ○ smeared   ○ rain

> **Tip**
> A possessive noun shows ownership by a person, a place, or a thing.

© Harcourt

Directions

Look at the sentence in the box. The sentence has two mistakes in capital letters, punctuation, or grammar. Find the two mistakes and correct them. Mark through each mistake or use editing marks. If needed, write the correction above the mistake.

9 | The Fire alarm rung loudly in the hallway. | fire, rang

Directions In the sentence below, which pronoun **best** replaces the underlined words?

10 <u>My sister and I</u> shopped for clothes at the mall.

- ○ She
- ◉ We
- ○ They
- ○ Us

> **Tip**
> When choosing a pronoun, think about how many people or things you are replacing.

Directions What change should be made to the sentence below?

11 Last night, Kim watch the team win their first game.

- ○ change <u>win</u> to <u>winned</u>
- ○ change <u>game</u> to <u>games</u>
- ○ change <u>Last</u> to <u>Lasted</u>
- ◉ change <u>watch</u> to <u>watched</u>

> **Tip**
> The words *last night* will help give you clues about the mistake in this sentence.

© Harcourt

STOP

Name _____

Directions

Read this fable about helping others. Then answer Questions 1 through 4. You may look back at the fable.

The Dove and the Ant

by Aesop

An Ant, feeling thirsty, went down to the river. She was leaning over to take a drink when she fell in! The rushing river carried her swiftly downstream. It seemed as if the Ant would surely drown.

A Dove on the bank of the river saw what was happening. He was a kind-hearted bird. He felt sorry for the tiny Ant. Finding a small branch, he threw it into the river and called to the Ant to grab hold of it. By this means, the Ant was able to reach the shore safely. She thanked the Dove and went on her way.

A little while later, however, the Ant came upon a hunter. She saw that the hunter was aiming his gun at the kind Dove who had saved her life. The Ant wanted to help her friend, but what could a tiny ant do?

In an instant, the Ant scurried up to the man. She bit him on the ankle as hard as she could. The sharp sting made the hunter stop to scratch, and so the Dove's life was saved.

MORAL: Little friends may turn out to be great friends.

Tip
This passage is a fable. In a fable, animals often take on human traits. As you read, notice how the characters have human thoughts, ideas, and feelings.

Tip
Look for time-order phrases in this passage to help you understand when events happen in the story.

© Harcourt

1 After getting out of the river, what problem does the Ant have to solve?

← Tip
Think about the most exciting part of the story. What was the Ant trying to do?

- ● She has to save the Dove from the hunter.
- ○ She has to find something to eat.
- ○ She has to get the Dove out of the river.
- ○ She has to learn to fly.

2 What happens <u>after</u> the Ant bites the man?

- ○ The man runs away.
- ● The man stops to scratch his ankle.
- ○ The Ant scurries to the Dove.
- ○ The man jumps into the river.

3 You find a book of fables in the library. Where would you look to see if <u>The Dove and the Ant</u> is one of the stories in the book?

- ○ title page
- ○ glossary
- ● table of contents
- ○ copyright page

4 Why is the Dove described in the fable as a kind-hearted bird?

← Tip
Find the place in the story where the Dove is described as kind-hearted. Think about the actions and words of the Dove. Do they help explain why the Dove is kind-hearted?

Answers will vary. Possible answers: The dove is

kind-hearted because he stops to help save the Ant.

Sometimes birds will eat insects, but the Dove does

not eat the Ant.

Directions

For Questions 5 through 7, read the story and look for the numbered, underlined parts. Choose the answer choices with the correct capital letters, punctuation, and grammar. If the underlined part is correct, mark "Correct."

Last <u>saturday,</u> the day began warm and sunny. Ryan <u>want to do</u> something
      (5)   (6)

fun. <u>He could go to the park. He could go to the pool.</u> It was a good day to be
                                (7)

outside.

5 ● Last Saturday

   ○ last Saturday

   ○ lasted Saturday

   ○ Correct

6 ○ wanting to do

   ○ wants doing

   ● wanted to do

   ○ Correct

7 **What is the best way to join these two sentences?**

   ● He could go to the park or the pool.

   ○ He could go to the park and go to the pool.

   ○ He could go to the park, but not the pool.

   ○ He could go to the park or could go to the pool.

> **Tip**
> When you join two sentences, write repeated words only once. Be careful that you don't change the meaning of the sentence.

8 **Which word in the sentence is an object pronoun?**

They wanted to give a prize to him.

   ○ they

   ○ to

   ○ prize

   ● him

> **Tip**
> An object pronoun usually appears in the predicate of a sentence.

© Harcourt

Directions

Look at the sentence in the box. The sentence has two mistakes in capital letters, punctuation, or grammar. Find the two mistakes and correct them. Mark through each mistake or use editing marks. If needed, write the correction above the mistake.

9 | We were served a delicious Breakfast earliest in the morning. | breakfast, early

Directions Choose the word that is spelled correctly.

10 The small bowl was filled with juicy _____.

- ○ berrys
- ○ berryes
- ● berries
- ○ berres

Tip
Think about the spelling rules when changing a noun that ends in -y to a plural form.

Directions How should the capitalization be corrected in the sentence below?

11 The train arrived in Jefferson city on Saturday, June 10.

- ○ change train to Train
- ○ change Jefferson to jefferson
- ● change city to City
- ○ change June to june

Tip
Proper nouns and the beginning word of a sentence need to be capitalized.

STOP

Directions

WRITE A PERSUASIVE PARAGRAPH   What is your favorite book of all time? Why do you love it so much? Write a paragraph about this book, telling your classmates why it is so great. Use the paragraph to try to convince them to read it.

Use the graphic organizer below to plan your persuasive paragraph. Then write the paragraph on a separate sheet of paper. When you are finished with the draft, use the Writing Checklist to revise and edit your work. Make a final copy of your story, and draw a picture of the book jacket to go with it.

My Favorite Book:

Why My Classmates Should Read It:

One Reason I Love This Book:

Another Reason I Love This Book:

A Third Reason I Love This Book:

© Harcourt

Conclusion:

Writing Checklist

❑ Did my first sentence clearly state which book is my favorite?

❑ Did I include three details that support my opinion?

❑ Did I use details that are related to the book's story?

❑ Did I use words and sentences that will convince my classmates to read it?

❑ Did I use pronouns correctly?

❑ Did I use capital letters and punctuation correctly?

❑ Did I spell words correctly?

❑ Did I use my best handwriting?

STOP

*D*irections

Read this poem about a special wish. Then answer Questions 1 through 4. You may look back at the poem.

A Wish

Saturday I flew my kite

on a hilltop high.

It leaped up like a dancer

and sailed across the sky.

When it dips and bobs along,

flying looks so easy!

I wish that I could soar like that

when the day is breezy.

1 **What is this poem mostly about?**

○ The writer wishes to fly a kite.

○ The writer wishes to become a dancer.

● The writer enjoys flying a kite.

○ The writer wishes for a new kite.

2 **What does the title tell you about the poem?**

○ The writer will tell about flying a kite.

● The writer has a wish.

○ The writer is very young.

○ The poem will tell a story.

Tip
Be sure to look at the title only when you choose your answer.

3 **In the poem, what do the words *dips* and *bobs* describe?**

● how the kite moves

○ how the kite feels

○ how the kite smells

○ how the kite sounds

Tip
Find the words *dips* and *bobs* in the poem and read the line that includes them. What are these words describing? Can you picture what these words describe in your mind as you make your choice?

4 **Using details from the poem, what was the weather like on that Saturday? Why do you think so?**

Answers will vary. Possible answer: I can tell the weather was breezy and it was probably sunny. I know this because the poem says the kite soars when the day is breezy and kites don't soar very well in the rain.

GO ON

*D*irections

For Questions 5 through 7, read the story and look for the numbered, underlined parts. Choose the answer choices with the correct capital letters, punctuation, and grammar. If the underlined part is correct, mark "Correct."

The Amusement park has a new roller coaster. These coaster has a
(5)   (6)
double loop in the middle. The new design is much fastest and safer than the
(7)
old one. I can hardly wait to ride it!

5 ○ amusement Park has

○ amusement park have

● amusement park has

○ Correct

6 ● This coaster

○ this coaster

○ Those coaster

○ Correct

7 ○ is much fast

○ is more fastest

● is much faster

○ Correct

8 Which word best completes the sentence?

Several boys are _____ across the field.

○ ran   ○ runs   ● running   ○ runing

> **Tip**
> The linking verb *are* is a clue to what verb you should choose.

© Harcourt

Directions

Look at the sentence in the box. The sentence has two mistakes in capital letters, punctuation, or grammar. Find the two mistakes and correct them. Mark through each mistake or use editing marks. If needed, write the correction above the mistake.

9 | The Family live in the blue house on the corner. |

family, lives

10 **Which underlined word is an adjective?**

- ● The <u>weary</u> traveler stopped to rest.
- ○ A drying wind blew across the <u>prairie</u>.
- ○ The sun <u>warmed</u> the brown earth.
- ○ Curious prairie dogs peered <u>out</u> of their burrows.

Tip
If you aren't sure if a word should be capitalized, ask yourself: Does the word name a person, a place, a thing, or an idea? Does the word begin a sentence? Is the word a special title?

Directions **How should the punctuation be corrected in the sentence below?**

11 **Ducks, fish frogs, and muskrats live in this pond.**

- ○ put a comma after <u>live</u>
- ● put a comma after <u>fish</u>
- ○ put a comma after <u>this</u>
- ○ put a comma after <u>muskrats</u>

Tip
Try placing a comma as each answer choice suggests. Then read the sentence aloud, pausing at each comma. Which choice sounds correct?

STOP

Directions

Read this Native American folktale about the antics of Coyote and Eagle. Then answer Questions 1 through 4. You may look back at the selection.

Coyote and Eagle Steal the Sun and Moon: A Zuni Folktale

Long ago, the land was always dark, and it was summer all the time. One day, Eagle and Coyote went out to hunt for food. Coyote was not a very good hunter because he couldn't see well in the dark.

After a while, Eagle and Coyote came to the home of the Kachinas. The Kachina people were very powerful. They had a shining box that held the sun and the moon.

Eagle and Coyote wanted the shining box. They wanted to use its shining light to help them hunt in the dark. "Let us wait until the Kachinas have gone to sleep," said Eagle. "Then we can take the box and run away." So that's what they did.

Coyote was curious. He wanted to see what was in the box. But at first, Eagle carried the box. He carried it a long way. "Eagle, my friend," said Coyote. "Why not let me carry the box for a while?"

"No, no," said Eagle. "I can carry it."

A little while later, Coyote again asked to carry the box. Again Eagle refused. But Coyote kept offering and asking and begging to carry the box until at last Eagle gave in.

Coyote thought it wouldn't hurt to take a peek inside the box. So he tipped open the lid just a little bit.

Out flew the sun and the moon! Up to the sky they flew!

From that day on, the sun and moon remained in the sky and gave light to the land below. But because they flew so far away, the land had less heat. So now we have winter for part of every year.

> **Tip**
> The Zuni are a Native American people of New Mexico and Arizona. Animals and nature are important elements in Zuni stories.

> **Tip**
> When you come to a long word such as *Kachina*, look for the syllables in the word. Notice that it begins with a capital letter. Read the words around it to help you figure out what it means.

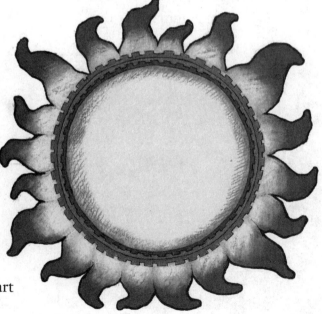

© Harcourt

---

1 What does this folktale explain?

   ○ why Coyote is curious

   ○ why we have darkness

   ○ how Coyote played a trick on Eagle

   ● how the sun and the moon got in the sky

> **Tip**
> This folktale tells how or why something is the way it is. Reread the ending carefully to find what this folktale explains.

2 How is the land different at the end of the story than it was at the beginning?

   ○ It is dark all the time, and winter comes for part of the year.

   ○ It is light all of the time.

   ○ It is winter all of the time.

   ● It isn't always summer, and during the day it is light.

> **Tip**
> Reread the descriptions of the land at the beginning and end of the folktale to see how the land is different.

3 Who could not see well in the dark?

   ○ Eagle

   ○ Kachina

   ● Coyote

   ○ Zuni

4 Why does Coyote want to carry the box?

Answers will vary. Possible answer: Coyote wants to

carry the box because he is curious. He wants to

know what is inside the box.

Directions

For Questions 5 through 7, read the story and look for the numbered, underlined parts. Choose the answer choices with the correct capital letters, punctuation, and grammar. If the underlined part is correct, mark "Correct."

<u>a Diamond</u> is a hard mineral. It can be used to cut <u>other minerals diamonds</u> are
      (5)   (6)

used on the blades of tools for cutting. Diamonds <u>are useful</u> as well as beautiful.
                                                                                    (7)

5 ○ A Diamond

   ○ An diamond

   ◉ A diamond

   ○ Correct

6 ○ other Minerals. diamonds

   ◉ other minerals. Diamonds

   ○ other minerals, Diamonds

   ○ Correct

7 ○ is useful

   ○ am useful

   ○ was useful

   ◉ Correct

> **Tip**
> Check whether the subject is singular or plural. This can help you decide which linking verb is correct.

8 Which choice <u>best</u> completes the sentence below?

   _____ a single bloom on that rose bush.

   ○ There are

   ◉ There is

   ○ They're are

   ○ They're is

> **Tip**
> Remember that an apostrophe is used in a contraction to show where letters have been removed. What two words does the contraction stand for? Does the contraction seem correct?

© Harcourt

*D*irections

Look at the sentence in the box. The sentence has two mistakes in capital letters, punctuation, or grammar. Find the two mistakes and correct them. Mark through each mistake or use editing marks. If needed, write the correction above the mistake.

9 | Last night, a light drizzle begin to fall from the clouds over Mount tallac.

began, Tallac

Directions What is the simple subject in the sentence below?

10 Six mallard ducks waddled quickly across the lawn.

- ○ six mallard ducks
- ○ mallard ducks
- ● ducks
- ○ waddled

11 Which one is *not* a complete sentence?

- ● Seen across the distant hills.
- ○ A rainbow appeared behind the clouds.
- ○ The night sky was full of stars.
- ○ Rain falls silently.

Tip
A sentence needs both a subject and a predicate in order to be complete.

© Harcourt

STOP

D*irections*

Read this African folktale about how the crocodile got his bumpy back. Then answer Questions 1 through 4. You may look back at the selection.

Why the Crocodile Has a Bumpy Back: A Folktale from Angola

Long ago, the crocodile's back was as soft and smooth as a little child's. One afternoon, the crocodile was taking a nap beside the river. Suddenly, the rabbit came dashing along and bumped right into him.

"Rabbit," said the crocodile, "why did you wake me? And why are you all out of breath?"

"I have been running all morning from the dog," the rabbit panted. "A man sent him to chase me. I think the man wants to have me for his dinner!" Suddenly, the rabbit had a thought that made him nervous. "You're not hungry, are you?" he asked the crocodile.

Tip
What makes Rabbit nervous? Use clues from the folktale and your own knowledge to decide.

"No," said the lazy crocodile. "I've already had my dinner."

"That's good," said the rabbit with a sigh of relief. "I've had enough trouble for one day."

"Well," said the crocodile, "I never have trouble. In fact, I bet Trouble would be afraid to bother me."

"I don't think you should talk like that," the rabbit warned him. "Trouble might not like you to talk about him that way."

The rabbit hopped off, but the crocodile could not stop thinking about what he had said. The more he thought, the more angry he became. At last, he decided to go find Trouble and tell him to mind his own business.

The crocodile frightened the flamingo, who was wading in the river. She flew up in the air and startled the monkey, who had just lit the candles on his birthday cake. The monkey jumped away to hide, knocking over the birthday cake and setting fire to the tall, dry grass.

Tip
These two paragraphs tell a sequence of events that leads to the story's conclusion. Read slowly so you understand how one event leads to the next.

As the flames grew higher and higher around him, the crocodile ran to throw himself in the river. By the time he reached the safety of the cool water, his back was burned and rough. Ever since then, the crocodile's back has been bumpy, and he's been a grumpy fellow.

© Harcourt

1 **According to this tale, why does the crocodile have a bumpy back?**

- ● The crocodile gets burned.
- ○ The crocodile is grumpy.
- ○ The crocodile is very old.
- ○ The crocodile is not hungry.

2 **Why doesn't the crocodile eat the rabbit?**

- ● He had already eaten.
- ○ He thinks rabbits taste bad.
- ○ He is afraid of Trouble.
- ○ Rabbits have too much fur.

Directions: **Read this sentence from the folktale.**

> He decided to go find Trouble and tell him to mind his own business.

3 **What does this sentence mean?**

- ● Trouble should leave the crocodile alone.
- ○ Trouble should start rabbit hunting with the crocodile.
- ○ Trouble should open a business and make money.
- ○ Trouble needs to watch over the crocodile's children.

Tip

It may be necessary for you to reread this sentence, and the sentences that surround it, to find out what the crocodile means.

4 **Here are some events from the folktale. Place the events in order from 1 to 4 by writing the numbers in the boxes next to each sentence.**

- 2 The crocodile goes looking for Trouble.
- 1 The rabbit wakes the crocodile.
- 4 The birthday cake sets the grass on fire.
- 3 The crocodile scares the flamingo.

Tip

Find each of these events in the folktale again. Keep track of the order in which they appear before you number the sentences.

© Harcourt

Directions

For Questions 5 through 7, read the story and look for the numbered, underlined parts. Choose the answer choices with the correct capital letters, punctuation, and grammar. If the underlined part is correct, mark "Correct."

Jeffrey wanted to go to <u>the game? Before</u> he could leave, he had to finish his
$$(5)$$
homework. He was <u>ready to going</u> only fifteen minutes later. He didn't realize he
$$(6)$$
could finish <u>so quick!</u>
$$(7)$$

5 ● the game. Before
   ○ the game before
   ○ the Game. Before
   ○ Correct

> **Tip**
> A question has a different structure than other sentences and asks for information. Questions often use words like *who, what, which, where, why, when,* and *how.*

6 ○ ready to gone
   ● ready to go
   ○ ready to went
   ○ Correct

7 ● so quickly!
   ○ so quicker!
   ○ so quickest!
   ○ Correct

> **Tip**
> Remember that adverbs tell more about a verb. What do many adverbs have as a suffix?

8 Read the sentence and choose the correct punctuation mark.

   How many people know where the key is

   ○ !   ● ?   ○ ( )   ○ .

GO ON

Directions

Look at the sentence in the box. The sentence has two mistakes in capital letters, punctuation, or grammar. Find the two mistakes and correct them. Mark through each mistake or use editing marks. If needed, write the correction above the mistake.

9 | Colorfull banners fluttered, softly in the breeze.

colorful, delete comma

Directions: Which word in the sentence below should be capitalized?

10 The Founder's Day parade took place on thursday, April 16.

- ◯ place
- ⬤ thursday
- ◯ took
- ◯ parade

Directions: Which words best fill in the blanks in the sentence below?

11 Jamie _____ the heavy _____ of the drums.

- ◯ *herd* and *beat*
- ⬤ *heard* and *beat*
- ◯ *heard* and *beet*
- ◯ *herd* and *beet*

Tip
All the words in the answer choices are spelled correctly. Some words sound the same, but have different meanings depending on their spellings. Which spellings match the words' meanings in the sentence?

© Harcourt

STOP

Directions

Read this Native American story about a young girl. Then answer Questions 1 through 4. You may look back at the selection.

Oochigeaska: A Cinderella Story of the Mik'maq Indians

Tip

As you read, compare this story to the Cinderella story you know. Think about the ways the two stories are similar.

In a village at the edge of a lake lived a great hunter. He was invisible to everyone but his sister. It was said that he would marry any other girl who could see him.

Many girls came to visit the invisible hunter and his sister. The sister would ask, "Do you see my brother's sled strap? Do you see his bow-string?"

Some said they could see them. But when the sister asked what the sled strap and bow-string were made of, no one ever gave the right answer. So the sister knew they didn't really see him.

Tip

Look for details in this story that help you picture items that are a part of the Mik'maq Indian culture.

In the village there lived an old man who had three daughters. The older daughters always made fun of the youngest one. They made her do all the work. They called her Oochigeaska, "burnt-skin girl," because her face was darker than theirs from working under the hot sun every day.

One day Oochigeaska got the idea in her head to go to the wigwam of the invisible hunter to try her luck. Because her clothes were all in rags, she made herself a dress, cap, and leggings of birch bark. Her sisters laughed at her and called her names, but she was determined to go.

The sister of the invisible hunter was kind to the girl. She took her down to the lake where her brother was and asked, "Do you see him?"

"I do!" Oochigeaska exclaimed.

"What is his sled strap made of?" the sister asked.

"It is the rainbow," Oochigeaska replied.

"And what is his bow-string?" asked the sister.

"It is the stars in the northern sky," said Oochigeaska.

Then the sister knew that Oochigeaska truly could see him. She took Oochigeaska home and washed her. Her hair grew long and shiny as a blackbird's wing, and her eyes twinkled like stars.

So the invisible hunter married Oochigeaska, and she sat in the wife's seat in his wigwam all the rest of her days.

© Harcourt

1 What does the name *Oochigeaska* mean?

  ○ Cinderella

  ● burnt-skin girl

  ○ rainbow

  ○ oldest daughter

2 How are Oochigeaska and Cinderella alike?

  ● Both are treated badly by their sisters.

  ○ Both meet an invisible man.

  ○ Both have a fairy godmother.

  ○ Both make clothes of birch bark.

Tip
Read each choice carefully. Choose the one that is the same for both stories, not just one.

3 You are reading a book called *American Indian Legends* and you want to know when the book was published. Where in the book should you look?

  ○ table of contents

  ● copyright page

  ○ index

  ○ glossary

Tip
Think about the features of each part of the book. Which one contains publishing information?

4 How can you tell that Oochigeaska is a creative person?

  Answers will vary. Possible answer: I can tell that

  Oochigeaska is creative because she makes new

  clothes from birch to replace her old torn clothing.

Directions

For Questions 5 and 6, read the story and look for the numbered, underlined parts. Choose the answer choices with the correct capital letters, punctuation, and grammar. If the underlined part is correct, mark "Correct."

A soft rain begans to fall. Wet raindrops glistened. on the leaves.
                    (5)   (6)
The grass was wet and shiny. A mist seemed to hang from the clouds
                    (7)
like a giant curtain.

5 ○ beginning to fall

⬤ began to fall

○ began to falling

○ Correct

6 ○ glistened, on

⬤ glistened on

○ glistened. On

○ Correct

7 **Which of the following sentences would be a more detailed replacement for sentence 7?**

⬤ Tiny diamond-like droplets sparkled on the grass.

○ The rain sounded like a drummer's beat.

○ Raindrops pounded the grass flat.

○ The grass was as green as a shamrock.

> **Tip**
> Details tell more about the subject in a sentence. They can help you picture in your mind what the writer wants you to see.

Directions Choose the word that is spelled correctly.

8 **The baby _____ because he was hungry.**

○ cryed

⬤ cried

○ cryd

○ criyed

> **Tip**
> When a verb ends in -y, what is the common spelling rule for making it past tense?

© Harcourt

*D*irections

Look at the sentence in the box. The sentence has two mistakes in capital letters, punctuation, or grammar. Find the two mistakes and correct them. Mark through each mistake or use editing marks. If needed, write the correction above the mistake.

9

> The amusement park was more crowdeder than it was last Week.

crowded, week

Directions Which change should be made to the sentence below?

10 Toby saw a animal scurry behind that rock.

- ● change *a* to *an*
- ○ change *saw* to *seen*
- ○ change *that* to *those*
- ○ change *scurry* to *scurries*

> **Tip**
> If you are unsure which change is correct, try each change in the sentence and read it aloud to yourself. Does one choice sound more correct than the others?

Directions What is the purpose of the sentence below?

11 This is the most exciting ride!

- ○ make a statement
- ○ ask a question
- ○ make a request
- ● state a strong feeling

> **Tip**
> The punctuation at the end of the sentence can give you clues about its purpose.

© Harcourt

STOP

Directions

Read this drama about how a shoemaker and some elves help each other. Then answer Questions 1 through 4. You may look back at the passage.

The Elves and the Shoemaker

CHARACTERS

Henry, the shoemaker   Second Elf

Polly, his wife   Third Elf

First Elf

SCENE 1: A cozy living room with a fire in the fireplace. Henry and Polly are sitting near the fire.

HENRY: Do you remember when we were so poor that I could buy leather for only one pair of shoes?

POLLY: How could I forget? You cut out the leather and left it on the workbench to finish in the morning.

HENRY: Yes, but in the morning the shoes were already made! So I bought more leather and cut it out, and the next morning we found two more pairs of shoes!

POLLY: I wonder who is helping us? Tonight let's hide in the workshop and see.

SCENE 2: A week later. The shoemaker's workshop. Henry and Polly are putting little pants, jackets, and hats on the workbench.

HENRY: You've been sewing these clothes ever since we hid in the workshop last week and saw the three little elves.

POLLY: I thought this would be a good way to repay them, as their clothes are so ragged and worn.

HENRY: They should be here any minute now. Let's hide. (They hide behind a curtain in the corner. A moment later, three elves enter the workshop.)

FIRST ELF: (Holding up a jacket) What's this? What a beautiful jacket! (He puts it on.) And it's just my size. Look here, fellows!

SECOND ELF: Here's a fine hat, with a nice long feather!

THIRD ELF: Look, there are pants and jackets and hats for all of us!

1 Why do you think the author wrote this drama?

- ● to entertain an audience with an enjoyable story
- ○ to persuade you to become a shoemaker
- ○ to give facts about elves
- ○ to give instructions for making shoes

2 How are Scene 1 and Scene 2 alike?

- ○ The elves are in both scenes.
- ○ The setting is the same in both scenes.
- ● Henry and Polly are in both scenes.
- ○ A visitor arrives in both scenes.

> **Tip**
> Compare the characters, setting, and actions of each scene before you make your choice.

3 Which of the following is the theme of the drama?

- ● Be kind to others, and they will be kind to you.
- ○ Judge someone by the kind of clothes they wear.
- ○ People who sew get rich quickly.
- ○ Elves like to wear nice things.

> **Tip**
> A story's theme is the "big idea" of a story. The theme can be an idea or belief about life, nature, and so on.

4 How can you tell the shoemaker and his wife are kind people?

Answers will vary. Possible answer: I can tell

they are kind because they do something nice for

the elves.

_____

© Harcourt

GO ON

Directions

For Questions 5 through 7, read the story and look for the numbered, underlined parts. Choose the answer choices with the correct capital letters, punctuation, and grammar. If the underlined part is correct, mark "Correct."

The Great plains is a large area of the United States. It is a grassy region.
      (5)   (6)

Nebraska, Kansas and Oklahoma are states found in this region.
                 (7)

5 ○ the Great Plains
  ○ the great Plains
  ● The Great Plains
  ○ Correct

Tip
Remember that a proper noun is the name of a person, a place, a thing, or an idea. When more than one word makes up the name, all of the words should be capitalized.

6 ○ United States it
  ○ United states. It
  ○ United States It
  ● Correct

7 ○ Nebraska Kansas and Oklahoma
  ● Nebraska, Kansas, and Oklahoma
  ○ Nebraska, Kansas, and Oklahoma,
  ○ Correct

Tip
Look carefully at the placement of the commas in each answer choice.

8 **What type of sentence is the one below?**

Please place the money in an envelope.

  ○ interrogative/question
  ○ declarative/statement
  ● imperative/request
  ○ exclamatory/exclamation

© Harcourt

Directions

Look at the sentence in the box. The sentence has two mistakes in capital letters, punctuation, or grammar. Find the two mistakes and correct them. Mark through each mistake or use editing marks. If needed, write the correction above the mistake.

9 | The Movie was so funny that we laugh for an hour. |

movie, laughed

Directions: Which form of the adjective best fills in the blank in the sentence below?

10 The old oak is the _____ tree in the park.

- ○ more taller
- ○ most tall
- ○ most tallest
- ● tallest

> **Tip**
> When comparing two things, use *-er* or *more.* When comparing three or more things, use *-est* or *most.*

Directions: What is the structure of the sentence below?

11 The library is at the end of the street.

- ○ an incomplete sentence
- ● a simple sentence
- ○ a run-on sentence
- ○ a compound sentence

> **Tip**
> Think about the features of each type of sentence choice given. Choose the one that best describes the sentence example.

© Harcourt

STOP

*D*irections

WRITE A STORY Imagine that you have been made the mayor of your town for one day. Just when you settle into your new job, your friends come to you with a problem that only a mayor can solve. What is the problem? What will you do to solve it? Tell how you solve the problem and save the day. Use dialogue to move the story along.

Use the story map below to plan your story. Then write the story on a separate sheet of paper. When you are finished with the draft, use the Writing Checklist to revise and edit your work. Make a final copy of your story, and draw a picture to go with it.

Characters:

Setting:

How the Story Begins (The Problem):

Main Events:

1.

2.

3.

How the Story Ends (The Solution):

© Harcourt

Writing Checklist

❏ Did I include a clear beginning, middle, and ending?

❏ Did I use descriptive details and adjectives that make my story interesting?

❏ Did I include dialogue to move the story along?

❏ Did I include a problem and a solution in my story?

❏ Did I use different kinds of sentences in my story?

❏ Did I correctly use punctuation and capital letters?

❏ Did I spell words correctly?

❏ Did I write neatly?

STOP

Directions
  Read this story about a special gift for a favorite teacher. Then answer
  Questions 1 through 4. You may look back at the story.

Mrs. Small's Gift

Jada and Catherine really liked their teacher, Mrs. Small.
Mrs. Small read stories better than anyone else.

When Mrs. Small said she would not be teaching next year,
Jada and Catherine knew that they would miss her.

"Let's get a present for her before she leaves," said Catherine.

Jada and Catherine searched all over the mall. They could not
find anything they liked.

"Let's look in just one more store," said Catherine.

They walked into the card store. On a tiny shelf there was a
statue of a woman reading to a group of children.

"This is perfect!" said Jada. "When Mrs. Small looks at this
statue, she will think of us."

Tip
Notice the details in the
story about Mrs. Small.
These character
details will help you
understand what
happens in the story.

Tip
This story uses
dialogue to move the
story along. Dialogue
is the exact words a
character says, and
they are set within
quotation marks.

© Harcourt

1 **Which of the following from the story expresses an opinion?**

⊙ Jada and Catherine search all over the mall.

⦿ Mrs. Small reads stories better than anyone else.

⊙ They walk into a card store.

⊙ Mrs. Small is not teaching next year.

> **Tip**
> An opinion is a statement that expresses someone's idea or feeling. An opinion is *not* necessarily a fact.

2 **Which word below is *not* a synonym for *find*?**

⊙ discover

⊙ detect

⊙ locate

⦿ lose

3 **In what way are Jada and Catherine alike?**

⊙ They both like basketball.

⊙ They both have brown hair.

⊙ They both have a book collection.

⦿ They both like Mrs. Small.

4 **Why is the statue a good choice for Mrs. Small?**

Answers will vary. Possible answer: The statue

shows a woman reading to a group of children.

This is a good gift because the girls liked the stories

Mrs. Small used to read to them.

> **Tip**
> Reread the sixth paragraph to recall what the statue looks like. Then think about Mrs. Small's talents. These two pieces of information are clues to the answer.

GO ON

Directions

For Questions 5 through 7, read the story and look for the numbered, underlined parts. Choose the answer choices with the correct capital letters, punctuation, and grammar. If the underlined part is correct, mark "Correct."

The bison provided <u>many things. For</u> the Plains Indians. The skin was used to
(5)

make clothing and tipi covers. The <u>bones was used</u> to fashion tools. The meat
(6)

and fat provided food. <u>Nothing went</u> to waste.
(7)

5 ○ many things? For

  ● many things for

  ○ Many things. For

  ○ Correct

6 ● bones were used

  ○ bones were using

  ○ bones used

  ○ Correct

7 ○ Nothing gone

  ○ Nothing go

  ○ Nothing going

  ● Correct

8 In the following sentence, which word is the verb?

Later that day, Gina laughed at the funny pictures.

  ○ that

  ● laughed

  ○ funny

  ○ later

> **Tip**
> Remember that a verb shows action.

© Harcourt

*D*irections

Look at the sentence in the box. The sentence has two mistakes in capital letters, punctuation, or spelling. Find the two mistakes and correct them. Mark through each mistake or use editing marks. If needed, write the correction above the mistake.

9 | Sometimes? I like to read a book owtdoors. |

delete question mark, outdoors

Directions: Choose the best way to correct the sentence below.

10 Teri and me shopped for new books.

○ change *Teri* to *teri*
○ change *shopped* to *shopping*
◉ change *me* to *I*
○ change *books* to *Books*

> **Tip**
> Try reading the sentence with each change to see which ones makes the most sense.

11 Which of the following is *not* a complete sentence?

◉ In answer to her very interesting question.
○ The boy raised his hand to speak.
○ Another teacher stood in the open doorway.
○ Please put the notebooks back on the bookcase.

> **Tip**
> A complete sentence needs a subject and a predicate. To help you find where the predicate begins, look for the verb.

© Harcourt

STOP

Directions

Read this selection about horses. Then answer Questions 1 through 4. You may look back at the selection.

Horses of the Old West

When we think about cowhands of the Old West, we usually picture them on horseback. Horses have been doing important work and helping people get from one place to another for thousands of years. Without them, cattle ranching in the Old West would not have been possible.

The Quarter Horse

Different types of horses are suited to different kinds of work. One kind of horse used by cowhands in America is called the quarter horse. This breed was developed in America in the early 1700s. Quarter horses were able to get a quick start and run very fast over a short distance. They got their name because they were used in races in which the horses ran a quarter mile.

Quarter horses proved to be useful for more than just racing. They could make quick turns and fast stops and starts. They were also quick to recognize and obey the slightest signals from their riders. These qualities made them ideal for ranch work, such as rounding up cattle or sorting out cattle from a herd. Cowhands rode quarter horses on long cattle drives, too, because the horses were steady on their feet and tough enough to keep going under difficult conditions.

Wild Horses of the West

Over the years, some of the cowhands' horses escaped or were set free. They joined bands of other tame horses that had once belonged to Spanish explorers and to Native Americans. The descendants of these horses were called mustangs, or wild horses. A hundred years ago, there were more than two million mustangs living free in parts of the western United States. Today, however, there are only about 20,000 left.

Tip
Pay attention to the title and subtitles in a nonfiction selection. They can help you predict what the main idea will be. The subtitles can also help you locate specific details after you read.

Tip
This paragraph gives many details about quarter horses. After you read this paragraph, paraphrase the details to remember them.

© Harcourt

1 **What is the main idea of this selection?**

◉ Horses did important work in the Old West.

○ Quarter horses run really fast.

○ Wild horses are called mustangs.

○ Cowhands had a difficult job in the Old West.

Tip
As you read the choices, be sure that the main idea is supported by details in all the paragraphs.

2 **How did the quarter horse get its name?**

○ In the Old West, a quarter horse only cost a quarter a day to feed.

○ A quarter horse is one quarter the size of a wild horse.

○ All quarter horses have spots the size of a quarter.

◉ Quarter horses were used in races a quarter mile long.

3 **Where did mustangs *most* likely come from?**

◉ They were horses that had escaped or were set free.

○ They traveled over the land bridge from Asia.

○ They traveled north from Mexico and Central America.

○ They were sold at an auction.

4 **Why is the quarter horse ideal for cowhands? Give two reasons.**

Answers will vary. Possible answer: Quarter horses

make quick turns and fast stops and starts for

steering. Also, they are steady on their feet and tough

for long cattle drives.

Tip
Be sure to tell how the quarter horse is ideal, giving a reason why this feature is a help to cowhands.

© Harcourt

Name _____

Directions

For Questions 5 through 7, read the story and look for the numbered, underlined parts. Choose the answer choices with the correct capital letters, punctuation, and grammar. If the underlined part is correct, mark "Correct."

William <u>waked up</u> very excited. Today <u>his Family</u> would make a trip to the
       (5)   (6)

zoo. They would have a picnic lunch in the <u>park nearby. They</u> had many
                                                  (7)

things planned.

5 ● woke up
  ○ wake up
  ○ woked up
  ○ Correct

6 ○ his Families
  ● his family
  ○ he family
  ○ Correct

> **Tip**
> Remember that a proper noun is the name of a specific person, place, or thing.

7 ○ park nearby, they
  ○ Park nearby. They
  ○ parked nearby. They
  ● Correct

8 Read the sentence and choose the correct punctuation mark.

Toby will ride his horse in the rodeo

  ○ ?
  ○ !
  ● .
  ○ "

© Harcourt

Name _____

Directions

Look at the sentence in the box. The sentence has two mistakes in capital letters, punctuation, or grammar. Find the two mistakes and correct them. Mark through each mistake or use editing marks. If needed, write the correction above the mistake.

9 | The cowboy always keep his Horse in the barn. |

keeps, horse

Directions: **Choose the answer that <u>best</u> completes the sentence.**

Tip
Does the word *keep* sound correct with the subject *cowboy*?

10 **The dancer _____ dreaming of her performance on stage.**

○ were
○ am
○ are
● was

Directions: **Choose the word that is an adjective in the sentence below.**

11 **The sequins on her costume sparkled in the bright lights.**

○ sequins
○ sparkled
● bright
○ lights

Tip
An adjective is a word that describes a noun.

© Harcourt

Lesson 22   103

Name _____

***D**irections*

Read this story about the building of the first railroad to cross the United States. Then answer Questions 1 through 4. You may look back at the story.

Working on the Railroad

Charles drove another spike into the ground. Then he stood up and wiped his brow. As far as he could see to the east or west, miles of railroad track stretched across the land. What a grand sight!

Like many young men in 1869, Charles was helping to build a railroad line that would connect the eastern United States with the western United States. All day long he drove metal spikes into the ground to keep the rails in place. It was backbreaking work, but Charles thought it was the best job in the world.

It was exciting to be taking part in such an important event in history. Very soon the final spike would be nailed into the ground. Then people could travel more rapidly and safely than ever before. This big country would seem like a much smaller place.

> **Tip**
>
> As you read, ask yourself questions, such as: How will the railroad change travel in the United States? What other effects will the railroad probably have?

© Harcourt

1 Read the second paragraph. What does *backbreaking* mean?

- ○ easy most of the time
- ● difficult and tiring
- ○ crushing one's bones
- ○ enjoyable

Tip

This term is an exaggeration. It is used to create an image in your mind. What do you think it really means? Use word clues from the story to find out.

2 Which statement states a fact?

- ● Miles of railroad track stretched across the land.
- ○ Charles had the best job in the world.
- ○ It was exciting to be a part of this important event.
- ○ The miles of track were a grand sight.

Tip

Remember that a *fact* is a statement that can be proven. Statements that tell what someone thinks or feels are *opinions*, not facts.

3 What can you *probably* predict happened after the railroad was completed?

- ○ It was easier to go across the sea.
- ● Travel was faster across the United States.
- ○ People preferred to walk across the United States.
- ○ The trains did not work properly.

Directions Read this sentence from the story.

> This big country would seem like a much smaller place.

4 What does this sentence mean?

Answers will vary. Possible answer: This sentence

means that it would be easier and faster to travel

across the country so it would seem smaller. The

country wouldn't actually be any smaller.

© Harcourt

Name _____

Directions

For Questions 5 through 7, read the story and look for the numbered, underlined parts. Choose the answer choices with the correct capital letters, punctuation, and grammar. If the underlined part is correct, mark "Correct."

Saturday was the first really nice day of spring. <u>Dad wanted we</u> to help him in the
(5)

yard. I picked up sticks on the lawn. <u>Jessie helped Dad</u> carry out the lawn chairs.
(6)

Mom planted <u>some flower in pots</u>. Now we were ready for more good weather.
(7)

5 ○ dad want we

  ○ Dad wants we

  ● Dad wanted us

  ○ Correct

6 ○ Jessie helped dad

  ○ Jessie helping Dad

  ○ jessie helped dad

  ● Correct

7 ● some flowers in pots

  ○ some flower on pots

  ○ a flowers in pots

  ○ Correct

> **Tip**
> When a common noun is used as a name to address a person, it needs to be capitalized like a proper noun. Read the sentence carefully to see if the noun is used as someone's name.

Directions **Choose the word that is spelled correctly.**

8 My brother set _____ of grapes on the table.

  ○ bunchs

  ● bunches

  ○ bunchez

  ○ buntches

> **Tip**
> Think about the rules of spelling you know when you are looking at a plural noun.

© Harcourt

Name _____

Directions

Look at the sentence in the box. The sentence has two mistakes in capital letters, punctuation, or grammar. Find the two mistakes and correct them. Mark through each mistake or use editing marks. If needed, write the correction above the mistake.

9 | Cory wanted to by peaches, strawberries, and plums, for lunch. |

buy, delete last comma

Directions Choose the answer that is the complete subject of the sentence below.

10 **My tired eyes could not focus on the target.**

   ○ eyes

   ○ tired eyes

   ● My tired eyes

   ○ target

> **Tip**
> To find the subject, ask yourself who or what is performing the action.

Directions Choose the word that <u>best</u> completes the sentence below.

11 **I watch quietly while Mama _____ berries at the edge of the woods.**

   ○ pickes

   ○ pick

   ○ picking

   ● picks

> **Tip**
> Read carefully to figure out who or what is performing this action. Then think about how the verb needs to agree with the noun.

STOP

Directions

Read this story about a girl's experience with Japanese puppets. Then answer Questions 1 through 4. You may look back at the story.

The Bunraku Puppets

Aliza was excited. Today her school had special visitors. They were people from Japan who acted out a story with puppets, called Bunraku puppets. The puppets were about half the size of a real person.

Aliza watched carefully as three people moved one puppet around. The chief puppeteer moved the head, the different parts of the face, and the right arm and hand. The other two puppeteers moved the rest of the puppet. While the puppets moved, another man sat on the stage in a beautiful costume. He told the story. He talked for the puppets and gave them feelings. He cried, shouted, whispered, and laughed.

When the play was over, Aliza's teacher took the students backstage to meet the puppeteers and see the puppets. The chief puppeteer showed Aliza how he made the puppet's head move through an opening in the back of the puppet's costume.

Aliza loved the puppets, which almost seemed like real little people. She decided that one day she would like to visit Japan and see the famous National Bunraku Theater.

> **Tip**
> The word *Bunraku* is probably new to you. Read the story to find out what Bunraku puppets are.

> **Tip**
> This paragraph gives details about how the puppets work. Slow down to read the details carefully and visualize in your mind what is happening.

© Harcourt

1 **How does the author contrast the puppets with real people?**

Tip
Remember that to contrast two things, you think about how they are different from each other.

○ The puppets and puppeteers are all from Japan.

○ Real people make the puppets move and talk.

● The puppets are about half the size of real people.

○ The puppets come alive at the end of the play.

2 **Describe how people operate the Bunraku puppets.**

Answers will vary. Possible answer: One person

moves the head, face, and right arm and hand of the

puppet. Two more people move all the other parts of

the puppet. Another person sits on the stage and

does the voices of the puppets.

3 **Aliza wants to read more about Bunraku puppets. She chooses a book called *Making and Performing with Puppets*. Where can she look to see if this book contains any information about Bunraku puppets?**

○ title page

○ glossary

● index

○ copyright page

4 **Based on how it is used in the selection, what is a *puppeteer*?**

Tip
The suffix *eer* is a clue to what *puppeteer* means. Think of words like *pioneer* and *volunteer*. Do they describe people, places, or things?

○ a Japanese puppet

● a person who makes the puppet move

○ a wooden ear

○ a puppet stage

© Harcourt

Directions

Look at the sentence in the box. The sentence has two mistakes in capital letters, punctuation, or spelling. Find the two mistakes and correct them. Mark through each mistake or use editing marks. If needed, write the correction above the mistake.

5 | The ship's cook fryed our Breakfast over the open fire. |

fried, breakfast

Directions Choose the answer that best describes the underlined word.

6 A tropical breeze blew through the <u>trees</u> on Jamaica.

- ● a plural noun
- ○ a proper noun
- ○ a pronoun
- ○ an adjective

Tip
Think about the definitions for each answer choice. Then look at the underlined word.

7 Which sentence below has a verb written in the past tense?

- ○ Jamie sits quietly in the bow.
- ○ Soon the tide will roll into the harbor.
- ● The rowboat floated away from the dock.
- ○ We are playing with seashells in the sand.

Tip
Remember that past-tense verbs show action that has already happened.

© Harcourt

Name _____

Directions

For Questions 8 through 10, read the story and look for the numbered, underlined parts. Choose the answer choices with the correct capital letters, punctuation, and grammar. If the underlined part is correct, mark "Correct."

It was cold and rainy outside. Paula decided to make cinnamon rolls. <u>She taked</u>
(8)
frozen bread dough out of the freezer to thaw. Paula rolled out the dough and
spread it with melted <u>butter cinnamon, and sugar.</u> Then she rolled it up and cut it
(9)
into pieces. Finally, she was ready to bake the rolls <u>in the oven,</u>
(10)

8 ○ she took
○ She taking
● She took
○ Correct

9 ○ butter cinnamon and sugar
● butter, cinnamon, and sugar
○ butter, cinnamon. And sugar
○ Correct

> **Tip**
> Think about the rules of punctuation to follow when you are looking at a series of items.

10 ● in the oven.
○ in the oven?
○ on the oven.
○ Correct

11 Choose the word that <u>best</u> completes the sentence below.

Yesterday we _____ all the way across the harbor.

● paddled   ○ paddling   ○ paddle   ○ paddles

> **Tip**
> Look for time-order words in the sentence to help you choose the proper verb form.

STOP

Name _____

Directions
    Read this selection about a famous photographer. Then answer Questions 1 through 4. You may look back at the selection.

Dorothea Lange

Dorothea Lange was a famous photographer. She traveled all over the United States and to many other parts of the world taking photographs.

Her Early Life

Her early life was not easy. Born in New Jersey in 1895, she became ill with polio when she was seven years old. When Dorothea was twelve, she moved to her grandmother's home in the Harlem neighborhood of New York City with her mother and brother. There she graduated from high school and attended a training school for teachers.

Tip
Each subtitle shows where a new section of the selection begins. The subtitle gives you clues to what each section is about.

Her Career Begins

While Dorothea was going to school, she got her first job, working for a famous photographer. She was twenty-one years old when she began her own career as a photographer. She needed a darkroom, so she built one out of a chicken coop behind her home!

Tip
Words like *so* and *because* indicate a cause and effect. What did Dorothea build? Why did she build it?

Dorothea spent time traveling in the western United States with her first husband, who was a painter. One of her famous photographs, called "Hopi Indian," was taken during a trip to the Navajo and Hopi lands.

The Great Depression

Beginning in 1929, many people in the United States lost their jobs. Dorothea took photographs that showed this hard time in American history, which was called the Great Depression. One of those famous photographs, called "Family on the Road," was taken in Oklahoma. Dorothea also worked on a government project to help people find jobs.

Her Later Years

In later years, Dorothea's travels took her to Asia, South America, and Africa. Her photographs were exhibited, or shown, in Boston and in Europe. She died in 1965. In 1966, her photographs were exhibited at the Museum of Modern Art in New York City.

© Harcourt

1 **What is the main idea of the fifth paragraph?**

    ○ The Great Depression is a weather pattern that brings rain.

    ○ Dorothea preferred to take pictures of children and animals.

    ● The Great Depression had an effect on many people, including Dorothea.

    ○ Dorothea went on the road to sell her photographs.

> **Tip**
> Read the fifth paragraph carefully. Choose the answer that best describes what this paragraph is mostly about.

2 **What happened because Dorothea needed a darkroom?**

    ○ She paid a man to build her a darkroom.

    ● She turned an old chicken coop into a darkroom.

    ○ She quit taking pictures because she didn't have one.

    ○ She helped people find jobs building darkrooms.

3 **In which section would you look to find out about Dorothea Lange's childhood?**

    ● Her Early Life

    ○ Her Career Begins

    ○ The Great Depression

    ○ Her Later Years

> **Tip**
> Each answer choice is a subheading in the selection. Read the words in each subheading for clues to the correct answer. You can also skim each paragraph to see which one has details about her childhood.

4 **Here are some events from the selection. Place the events in order from 1 to 4 by writing the numbers in the boxes next to each sentence.**

    [2] Dorothea took the photograph titled "Hopi Indian."

    [4] Dorothea Lange died in 1965.

    [1] Dorothea attended a training school for teachers.

    [3] Dorothea worked on a government project to help people find jobs.

Directions

For Questions 5 and 6, read the story and look for the numbered, underlined parts. Choose the answer choices with the correct capital letters, punctuation, and grammar. If the underlined part is correct, mark "Correct."

Steamed artichokes are a favorite vegetable <u>for many People</u>. First of all, they
                                                        (5)

are <u>easy to prepared</u>. They taste good with melted butter. Artichokes are filling,
        (6)

too. _____
        (7)

5 ○ four many people

● for many people

○ for many peoples

○ Correct

6 ○ easy. To prepare

● easy to prepare

○ easy to prepares

○ Correct

Directions: For question 7, look at the paragraph above. Which sentence would be the <u>best</u> closing sentence for the paragraph?

7 ○ Carrots are also a favorite vegetable.

● It is easy to see why many people like artichokes.

○ I don't like vegetables.

○ Artichokes are a member of the thistle family.

> **Tip**
> Remember that a closing sentence often summarizes the details in a paragraph.

8 Choose the word that <u>best</u> completes the sentence.

Grandmother _____ me a story when she gets here.

○ tell   ● will tell   ○ told   ○ telling

> **Tip**
> Try reading this sentence with each answer choice. Read the entire sentence and look for word clues that can help you choose the correct answer.

© Harcourt

Name _____

Directions

Look at the sentence in the box. The sentence has two mistakes in capital letters, punctuation, or grammar. Find the two mistakes and correct them. Mark through each mistake or use editing marks. If needed, write the correction above the mistake.

9
> The teacher asked we to pay attention?

us, change ? to .

Directions Choose the words that best fill in the blanks in the sentence.

10 I watch my mother _____ the wheat _____ that she will use for the cake.

- ● *weigh* and *flour*
- ○ *weigh* and *flower*
- ○ *way* and *flower*
- ○ *way* and *flour*

> **Tip**
> Some words sound the same but have different spellings and meanings. Look carefully at the spellings. With which meaning does each belong?

11 Which of the following is an interrogative sentence?

- ● How many chocolates have you had?
- ○ You had more candies than I had.
- ○ I have not had any chocolates!
- ○ Show me where to find the candy.

> **Tip**
> An interrogative sentence asks a question.

© Harcourt

STOP

Directions

Think about a time when you, or someone in your family, won a contest or prize. Retell this event, using interesting details to build the same excitement that you felt during the event.

Use the space below to plan your personal narrative. Then write the story on a separate sheet of paper. When you are finished with the draft, use the Writing Checklist to revise and edit your work. Make a final copy of your story, and draw a picture to go with it.

Tip

You may want to use a story map to plan your personal narrative. List the characters and be sure to describe the setting in detail. Describe the main events in a logical order.

© Harcourt

Writing Checklist

❑ Be sure you wrote about winning a contest or prize.

❑ Create a narrative with a clear beginning, middle, and ending.

❑ Use vivid words to help build excitement.

❑ Use details to describe the setting and characters.

❑ Use a variety of complete sentences.

❑ Organize your story with transition or time-order words.

❑ Spell words correctly.

❑ Write clearly and neatly.

Tip

You want your audience to experience the excitement you felt. Use specific details and descriptive adjectives to help tell about this excitement.

Tip

The use of transition or time-order words, such as *first, next,* and *at last,* helps readers follow the sequence of events.

STOP

Directions
Read this poem about springtime. Then answer Questions 1 through 4.
You may look back at the poem.

Spring

The sky is bluebird blue.

The breeze blows warm and free.

Flowers grow and smell so sweet.

Grass makes a carpet under my feet.

The days go on.

The birds sing a song.

This is the best time for me.

Tip
As you read, pay attention to the rhythm and rhyme of the words.

Tip
What does the last sentence tell you about how the author feels about spring?

© Harcourt

1 Which statement below is *true* about the poem?

○ All of the lines rhyme at the end.

● Some of the lines rhyme at the end.

○ None of the lines rhyme at the end.

○ Only the first and last lines rhyme at the end.

Directions Read this line from the poem.

> Grass makes a carpet under my feet.

2 What does this line mean?

○ The grass turns into carpet.

○ Mr. Grass is a carpet maker.

○ It's easy to get grass on the carpet when you walk on it.

● The grass is thick and soft like a carpet.

Tip
The author uses figurative language— words that go beyond their everyday meaning—to help you make a picture in your mind.

3 Which sentence <u>best</u> summarizes the poem?

● Spring is the best season.

○ Birds make a lot of noise.

○ Flowers grow best in warm weather.

○ The days are long this time of year.

4 Why do you think the author wrote this poem?

Answers will vary. Possible answer: I think the author

wrote this poem to describe why he or she thinks

Spring is the best time.

_____

Tip
Your answer should include a purpose for the poem.

© Harcourt

Directions

For Questions 5 through 7, read the story and look for the numbered, underlined parts. Choose the answer choices with the correct capital letters, punctuation, and grammar. If the underlined part is correct, mark "Correct."

Calvary soldiers <u>had Special Jobs</u> to do. One job was to act as a lookout.

(5)

They also watched for <u>any strange activity's</u>. The calvary soldiers chased the

(6)

enemy that was in <u>retreat the job</u> of the calvary soldier was hard work.

(7)

5 ● had special jobs

○ had Special jobs

○ had special. Jobs

○ Correct

6 ○ any strange activitys

● any strange activities

○ any stranger activitys

○ Correct

7 ○ retreat the. Job

● retreat. The job

○ retreat? The job

○ Correct

8 Choose the word that <u>best</u> fills in the blank in the sentence below.

Last Saturday, my friends and I _____ to a free concert in the park.

○ go   ○ goes   ● went   ○ gone

Tip
Read carefully for time-order clues and the subject before you choose the correct verb form.

© Harcourt

*D*irections

Look at the sentence in the box. The sentence has two mistakes in capital letters, punctuation, or grammar. Find the two mistakes and correct them. Mark through each mistake or use editing marks. If needed, write the correction above the mistake.

9 | My father finded his new hammer, to be useful. |

found, delete comma

10 **Choose the sentence that is written correctly.**

- ● At the end of the year, Becky was the tallest person in class.

- ○ At the end of the year, Becky was the more tall person in class.

- ○ At the end of the year, Becky was the most tallest person in class.

- ○ At the end of the year, Becky was the most taller person in class.

> **Tip**
> Remember to use *more* or *-er* with an adjective when comparing two objects. Use *most* or *-est* with an adjective if comparing more than two objects.

11 **Write three simple sentences about your favorite time of the year. Capitalize and punctuate correctly.**

Answers will vary. Possible answer: Summer is my

favorite time of the year. The weather is very

warm. I go swimming every day.

_____

> **Tip**
> Read and follow the directions carefully. Be sure to include the correct number of sentences. Be sure they are simple sentences.

© Harcourt

STOP

Directions

   Read this selection about the rain forests. Then answer Questions 1 through 4.
   You may look back at the selection.

Rain Forests

Desert areas are mostly hot and dry. Rain forests are also
warm, but they are far from dry! Rain forests are wet areas of
vegetation, mostly near the equator in Central America, South
America, Africa, and Asia. The temperature in the rain forest
stays between 70 degrees and 85 degrees Fahrenheit, and rain
falls for part of every day.

The tall trees keep most of the sunlight from reaching the
ground, so the floor of the rain forest is dark. Because not much
light reaches the rain forest floor, very few plants grow there.
The plants that do grow there have very large leaves. These
leaves help the plants catch whatever light comes down through
the tall trees.

> **Tip**
> This paragraph lists a cause and effect. Why is the floor of the rain forest so dark? Find out what causes this effect to happen.

The Understory

The layer just above the forest floor is called the understory.
It reaches a level of forty or fifty feet above the ground. In the
understory, you can see the trunks of trees that reach toward
the top of the rain forest. This layer also has young trees and
shorter trees that can grow in the shade.

> **Tip**
> This selection explains the features of each layer of the rain forest. Pay attention to the details, but keep in mind that you can reread the subheadings and parts of the selection to locate information.

The Canopy

Above the understory is the canopy layer. The trees here grow
sixty to one hundred feet tall. Because they are very close
together, the tops of these trees form an almost solid
cover over the forest floor. The leaves and branches of
these trees shade the rest of the forest.

The Emergent Layer

Above the canopy is the emergent layer. Trees here are
more than one hundred feet tall. These trees are widely
separated. They are exposed to sun and wind all day.
There is very little animal life in this layer.

A Special Environment

Scientists believe that almost half of the earth's animals
and plants live in rain forests. Scientists who study life in rain
forests say that they have discovered only about one percent of
all the different kinds of animals and plants that live there.

1 **What causes the floor of the rain forest to be so dark?**

- ○ It rains there all the time.
- ● Tall trees keep out the sunlight.
- ○ Many plants grow there.
- ○ There are too many animals.

2 **Where are most rain forests located?**

- ○ in Africa
- ○ near the ocean
- ○ in the canopy layer
- ● near the equator

Directions: **Choose the word that has the *opposite* meaning of the underlined word.**

3 **exposed**

- ● hidden
- ○ separated
- ○ short
- ○ solid

> **Tip**
> Reread the fifth paragraph. What word might mean the *opposite* of *exposed* as it is described in this paragraph?

4 **Why do you think it is important that scientists study the rain forest?**

Answers will vary. Possible answer: Many kinds of

plants and animals live in the rain forest. Some of

these have not yet been discovered. Scientists could

discover important sources of food or medicine.

> **Tip**
> Base your answer on what you learn about rain forests in this selection as well as anything else you might already know. Be sure to use complete sentences.

*D*irections

Look at the sentence in the box. The sentence has two mistakes in capital letters, punctuation, or spelling. Find the two mistakes and correct them. Mark through each mistake or use editing marks. If needed, write the correction above the mistake.

5

> On February 16 2002, several familys went skiing on the mountain.

add comma after 16, families

Directions: Choose the word that best fills in the blank of the sentence below.

6 I _____ walking to school now.

- ○ are
- ● am
- ○ was
- ○ is

7 Which sentence below has an underlined noun?

- ○ Several <u>large</u> geese waddled to the pond.
- ○ A nest of eggs was <u>hidden</u> in the reeds.
- ○ The water lapped softly <u>against</u> the bank.
- ● Bright white clouds scuttled across the <u>sky</u>.

Tip
Which word names a person, a place, a thing, or an idea?

Directions

For Questions 8 and 9, read the story and look for the numbered, underlined parts. Choose the answer choices with the correct capital letters, punctuation, and grammar. If the underlined part is correct, mark "Correct."

July 15, 2003

Dear Mom,

Dad and me hiked five miles on the mountain today.
    (8)

We saw a deer and fawn. I took a picture for you.

Tomorrow we taked a canoe out on the lake.
         (9)

We miss you!

_____

         (10)
Toby and Dad

8 ○ dad and I

◉ Dad and I

○ Dad and you

○ Correct

9 ○ we will taking

◉ we will take

○ we took

○ Correct

> **Tip**
> Watch out for irregular verb forms and time-order clues in this sentence.

Directions: **Choose the answer that would best complete the letter above.**

10 ○ To Whom It May Concern,

◉ Love,

○ August 12, 2002

○ Dear Grandma,

> **Tip**
> Every letter needs a closing.

11 **Read the sentence and choose the correct punctuation mark.**

Set the table, please

○ ?   ◉ .   ○ ,   ○ "

STOP

Directions
   Read this selection about using a microscope. Then answer Questions 1
   through 4. You may look back at the selection.

Explore with Microscopes

Some people like to explore big places in the world, such as the
rain forest or the bottom of the ocean. Other people like to find
out about small things. What will you see if you cut open a
green pea? How can you find out what a cat hair really looks
like? The best way to find out about small things is to use a
microscope. Microscopes make tiny things look big.

Parts of a Microscope

Most microscopes have two lenses. Lenses are like mirrors
that magnify tiny things and make them look bigger. To use a
microscope, place what you want to look at on the flat surface.
The flat surface is called the "stage."

Light the Way

Lighting is important. The right lighting helps you see into
the tiny world on your stage. If the object you are looking at is
see-through, put a light under the stage. This way the light will
shine up through the object. If the object is not see-through,
put the light above the stage. Then the light will shine down on
the object.

Use the Microscope Properly

Place your eye against the eyepiece, and look through the
microscope. Use the big knob on the side of the tube to fix
the first focus. This moves the stage closer to the eyepiece or
farther away. Stop when the object looks almost clear. Then
twist the fine focus while you peer through the eyepiece again.
Keep fixing the fine focus until the object looks perfectly clear.
Now you can really explore this new, little world.

Tip
As you read this
paragraph, check
the diagram. The
diagram will help
you understand
what you are reading.

Tip
Scientific facts can be
hard to understand at
first. Slow down your
reading rate and think
about what the author
is telling you.

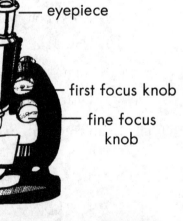

eyepiece

first focus knob

fine focus
knob

lenses

stage

mirror used
to reflect light

Name _____

1 According to the diagram, where is the first focus knob located?

- ○ on the lenses
- ○ under the mirror
- ○ below the stage
- ● on the side of the tube

Tip
The directions tell you that you need to look at the diagram in order to find your answer.

2 What happens when you turn the first focus knob?

- ● The stage moves closer or farther away.
- ○ The light shines through the object.
- ○ A mirror reflects your image.
- ○ The stage gets hot.

Tip
If you don't remember what will happen when you turn the knob, skim the selection until you find where it talks about the first focus knob. Then read carefully to find out what happens when you turn it.

3 Which of these should you do *after* you put an object on the stage?

- ○ Put the object in a test tube.
- ● Make sure that light is shining on the object.
- ○ Put the microscope away.
- ○ Call your friends to come and look.

4 List two reasons why people use microscopes.

1. Answers will vary. Possible answer: 1. People can use microscopes to look at small germs.

2. 2. Scientists can use microscopes to see what a small seed looks like.

GO ON ⟩

*D*irections

For Questions 5 through 7, read the story and look for the numbered, underlined parts. Choose the answer choices with the correct capital letters, punctuation, and grammar. If the underlined part is correct, mark "Correct."

Mr. Perry is <u>my favoritest teacher</u>. He likes to wear <u>funny ties he tells</u> us jokes
               (5)   (6)
to make us laugh. Best of all, <u>he makes us</u> feel like special people.
                               (7)

5 ● my favorite teacher
   ○ me favorite teacher
   ○ my more favorite teacher
   ○ Correct

6 ○ funny ties he. Tells
   ○ funny. Ties he tells
   ● funny ties. He tells
   ○ Correct

7 ○ he make us
   ○ he make we
   ○ him makes us
   ● Correct

Tip
Look for the correct pronoun to use as the subject and the object in a sentence. Then think about the correct verb to use with the subject pronoun.

Directions: Choose the word that is spelled correctly.

8 **I stopped writing _____ my hand was tired.**
   ● because   ○ beecuze   ○ becuze   ○ becouse

Tip
Some sight words are difficult to sound out. Does one of these look more correct than the others?

© Harcourt

GO ON ⟩

Directions

Look at the sentence in the box. The sentence has two mistakes in capital letters, punctuation, or spelling. Find the two mistakes and correct them. Mark through each mistake or use editing marks. If needed, write the correction above the mistake.

9 | Later that day we hiked allong the trail next to the stream. |

add comma after day, along

Directions: Choose the word that best completes the sentence.

10 This room feels _____ than the kitchen does.

- ● colder
- ○ more colder
- ○ coldest
- ○ most cold

Tip
When comparing two things, you often add *-er* to the adjective that is used to compare them. It is *never* correct to use *both more* and *-er* with the same adjective.

Directions: Choose the word that best replaces the underlined words.

11 <u>They are</u> planning a birthday party for their friend.

- ○ They's
- ○ They'll
- ○ They've
- ● They're

Tip
A contraction is made up of two words. Look at each answer choice and think of the two words that made that contraction. Which choice matches the underlined words?

© Harcourt

STOP

Directions

Read this letter about a trip to Switzerland. Then answer Questions 1 through 4. You may look back at the letter.

A Letter from Switzerland

Dear Denise,

I am having a wonderful time here in Switzerland. I wish you were here to see all the beautiful things I've been seeing.

Yesterday I went to Mount Rigi. Mount Rigi is near a beautiful city called Lucerne. In Lucerne, I paid for a ticket to ride a train up the mountain. At the very top of the mountain, we looked out. All around we could see the tops of very high mountains. The mountains are the Alps, and there is snow on them even though it is June!

Then the train went downhill for a little while. We got out on the side of the mountain. It was beautiful. The grass was very green. After a while, I took a cable car down the side of the mountain. You would have loved it!

Lots of love,

Aunt Theresa

Tip
Notice the form of this passage. Why is it written in this form?

Tip
This graph compares four mountains, one of which is in Switzerland, the country described in the passage. Although the graph is not referred to in the passage, it can help you understand the height of the world's tallest mountain compared to three other mountains around the world, including one in Switzerland.

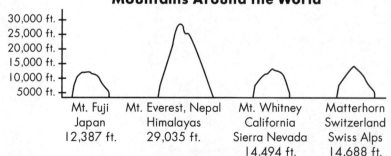

Mountains Around the World

30,000 ft.				
25,000 ft.				
20,000 ft.				
15,000 ft.				
10,000 ft.				
5000 ft.				

| Mt. Fuji Japan 12,387 ft. | Mt. Everest, Nepal Himalayas 29,035 ft. | Mt. Whitney California Sierra Nevada 14,494 ft. | Matterhorn Switzerland Swiss Alps 14,688 ft. |

© Harcourt

1 **Why is there snow on the mountain?**

○ because it is winter

● because the air stays colder at high altitudes

○ because ski resorts make snow

○ because the light plays funny tricks on the eyes

Tip
The article doesn't tell you exactly why there is snow. Use the information you learn in the article to draw a conclusion and choose the best answer.

2 **Which quote from the passage does *not* include an opinion?**

○ I am having a wonderful time here in Switzerland.

● I paid for a ticket to ride a train up the mountain.

○ Mount Rigi is near a beautiful city called Lucerne.

○ You would have loved it!

3 **According to the graph, which of the following statements is true?**

○ Mount Everest is roughly half the size of Mount Fuji.

● Mount Whitney is roughly half the size of Mount Everest.

○ Mount Fuji is taller than the Matterhorn.

○ Mount Whitney is taller than the Matterhorn.

4 **How can you tell that this passage is a letter?**

Answers will vary. Possible answer: I can

tell this is a letter because it begins with a greeting

and ends with a closing. It is from one person

to another.

Tip
Think about the features of a letter. Which of these features are shown in the passage? List these in your answer.

© Harcourt

Directions

Look at the sentence in the box. The sentence has two mistakes in capital letters, punctuation, or spelling. Find the two mistakes and correct them. Mark through each mistake or use editing marks. If needed, write the correction above the mistake.

5

the volcano to the south erupted last munth.

The, month

Directions Choose the word that has the same *root word* as the underlined word.

6 <u>disappearing</u>

- ○ pearl
- ◉ appearance
- ○ discover
- ○ diving

Tip
To find the root word, remove any prefixes and suffixes. The word that remains is the root word. The root word gives the word its meaning.

7 Write two compound sentences about a trip you really enjoyed. Capitalize and punctuate correctly.

Answers will vary. Possible answer: My family went to

Laguna Beach, and I attended the Art Festival. The

beach was very crowded, but I learned how to

body surf.

Tip
A compound sentence is made up of two simple sentences joined by the word *or*, *and*, or *but*.

© Harcourt

Name _____

*D*irections

For Questions 8 through 10, read the story and look for the numbered, underlined parts. Choose the answer choices with the correct capital letters, punctuation, and grammar. If the underlined part is correct, mark "Correct."

Mount St. Helens was once considered to be a dormant volcano. <u>Then, in 1980, it</u>
                                                                              (8)

erupted violently. Fully grown trees <u>was flattened</u> like toothpicks. Rivers and lakes
                                          (9)

were filled with ash. Now <u>Mount St. helens</u> is considered an active volcano, as
                              (10)

steam continues to rise from its core.

8 ○ Then in 1980 it

  ○ Then in, 1980 it

  ○ Then in, 1980, it

  ● Correct

> **Tip**
> Try reading each answer choice, pausing at the commas. Which way sounds best?

9 ● were flattened

  ○ were flatten

  ○ was flatten

  ○ Correct

10 ○ Mount St. helen's

  ○ mount St. Helens

  ● Mount St. Helens

  ○ Correct

> **Tip**
> All of the words that make up a proper noun should be capitalized.

11 **Choose the word that <u>best</u> replaces the underlined words in the sentence.**

  Theresa <u>will not</u> be attending the performance.

  ○ wasn't   ● won't   ○ weren't   ○ we'll

© Harcourt

STOP

Lesson 29   133

Directions

Read this selection about a famous inventor and astronomer. Then answer Questions 1 through 4. You may look back at the selection.

Galileo and the Skies

Galileo stared up at the night sky. He loved the lights that twinkled there. They looked so beautiful from where he stood. Since Galileo could not go to the stars and the moon, he found a way to bring the stars and planets closer.

Galileo heard of an inventor in Holland who had made a spyglass. A spyglass is a tool that helps people see faraway objects. He took that idea and made an even stronger spyglass. It was not strong enough to help him see the moon up close, though.

Finally, Galileo created a telescope that made things appear twenty times bigger than they really were. Galileo pointed his telescope toward the moon. He was amazed at what he saw! He discovered that there were mountains and cup-shaped holes, called craters, on the moon.

Galileo made other discoveries about the skies, too. His telescope showed him that the Milky Way was made of many, many stars. He also discovered the four largest moons of the planet Jupiter. He wrote about these discoveries in a book called *The Starry Messenger*.

> **Tip**
> Galileo doesn't actually bring the stars and moon closer to Earth. What does the author really mean by these words?

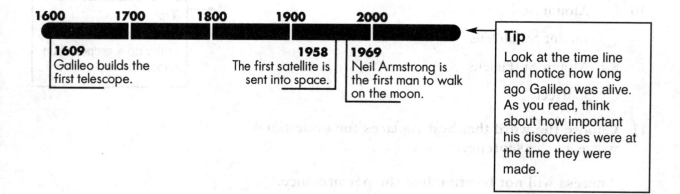

> **Tip**
> Look at the time line and notice how long ago Galileo was alive. As you read, think about how important his discoveries were at the time they were made.

© Harcourt

1 According to the time line, when did someone finally set foot on the moon? ◄

- ○ 1609
- ○ 1958
- ○ 1960
- ● 1969

Tip
To locate information on this time line, the numbers on top show the range of years on the time line. The numbers directly above each fact give the actual date that it happened.

2 What did Galileo do?

- ○ He invented the first spyglass.
- ○ He discovered the moon.
- ○ He walked on Mars.
- ● He invented a strong telescope.

3 What does the word <u>craters</u> mean in this selection? ◄

- ● cup-shaped holes
- ○ a box for shipping
- ○ stars in the Milky Way
- ○ people who make crayons

Tip
Reread the third paragraph. Sometimes an author tells the meaning of a word right in the sentence in which the word is used.

4 Why couldn't Galileo go to the moon?

Answers will vary. Possible answer: Galileo lived a

long time ago. Spaceships had not been invented yet.

There was no way for him to travel to the moon.

_____

© Harcourt

GO ON

Directions

For Questions 5 through 7, read the story and look for the numbered, underlined parts. Choose the answer choices with the correct capital letters, punctuation, and grammar. If the underlined part is correct, mark "Correct."

Sherry decided to planted some flowers. First, she dug a hole in the soil. Then,
            (5)

she took the plant out of the pot and loosened its roots next, she tucked the plant's
                                                        (6)

roots into the hole. To finish, sherry carefully firmed the soil around the plant.
                    (7)

5 ● decided to plant
   ○ decided planting
   ○ decided to plants
   ○ Correct

6 ○ Roots next,
   ○ roots next.
   ● roots. Next,
   ○ Correct

7 ○ To finish sherry,
   ● To finish, Sherry
   ○ To finish. Sherry
   ○ Correct

8 Choose the word that best fills in the blank in the sentence below.

   She is _____ in a clear, loud voice.

   ○ spoke   ● speaking   ○ speak   ○ spoken

   Tip
   What form of the verb often follows the helping verb *is*?

© Harcourt

*D*irections

Look at the sentence in the box. The sentence has two mistakes in spelling, punctuation, or grammar. Find the two mistakes and correct them. Mark through each mistake or use editing marks. If needed, write the correction above the mistake.

9 | The children had an appel in they're lunch bags. |

apple, their

Directions Choose the answer that <u>best</u> corrects the punctuation mistake in the sentence below.

10 Our soccer team has a game at Lincoln middle School. ←

○ put a capital *s* in *soccer*

● put a capital *m* in *middle*

○ put a small *l* in *Lincoln*

○ put a small *s* in *School*

Tip
Remember the rules for the capitalization of proper nouns.

11 Which sentence below is an exclamatory sentence? ←

● What an incredible performance that was!

○ Can you see the actors?

○ The actor spoke in a loud voice.

○ Please tell others about this fine show.

Tip
Think about what the punctuation mark is called at the end of each sentence. The name will help you find the answer.

© Harcourt

STOP

Directions

Imagine that you are almost asleep one night, when suddenly a huge meteor crashes into your backyard. Write about what happens that night and the next day.

Use the space below to plan your story. Then write the story on a separate sheet of paper. When you are finished with your draft, use the Writing Checklist to revise and edit your work. Make a final copy of your story, and draw a picture to go with it.

Tip

You may want to use a story map to plan your story. On the story map, list the characters, setting, problem, and solution. Place your story events in a logical order.

© Harcourt

Writing Checklist

❏ Be sure you wrote a story with a clear beginning, middle, and ending.

❏ Place the story events in a logical sequence.

❏ Present a problem that is solved at the end.

❏ Use descriptive language and vivid words that make your story interesting.

❏ Use a variety of sentence types and lengths.

❏ Check punctuation, capitalization, and spelling.

❏ Write a final copy that is neat and easy to read.

Tip
It is important that the events of the story follow a sequence that makes sense. If your story jumps around, your audience may get lost in what you are trying to say.

Tip
Vivid details about the characters, setting, and main events help the reader form a picture in his or her mind.

STOP

An Invitation

Dear Mrs. Connolly,

I am writing to ask you to come to the Winter Concert at Dove Springs Elementary School this weekend. My choir will sing in the concert, and some children will play songs on xylophones and cymbals.

You should come because the music will be wonderful. The choir and musicians have been practicing for six weeks. Also, all the performers will wear traditional costumes from other countries. We will look very interesting!

The concert is Saturday at 7 P.M. I hope you can come.

Your neighbor,

Julia

1. What is the purpose of the letter?
- ○ to ask Mrs. Connolly a question
- ○ to complain about rehearsals
- ● to persuade Mrs. Connolly to attend the show
- ○ to give directions to Julia's school

2. Which of these sentences from the letter is an opinion?
- ○ My choir will sing in the concert.
- ○ The performers will wear traditional costumes.
- ○ The concert is Saturday at 7 P.M.
- ● We will look very interesting!

STOP

The Frogs and the Well

by Aesop

Once there were two frogs who lived together in a swamp. One summer it got so hot that the swamp dried up. This made the two friends unhappy, as frogs usually prefer damp places. They decided to go out into the world and look for a new home.

The two frogs hopped about the countryside until at last they came to a well. The first frog peered down into the deep well. "This looks like a nice cool place," he said. "Let's jump in and make this our new home."

The other frog also looked down into the deep well. "Wait a minute, my friend," he said. "Let's give this some thought. Suppose this well dries up like the swamp did. How would we ever get out again?"

The first frog saw that his friend was right, and the two set off again in search of their new home.

MORAL: Look before you leap.

1. **What main problem do the characters face?**
   ○ They fall into a well.
   ● They need to find a new home.
   ○ They are thirsty and need water.
   ○ Their well has dried up.

2. **What might happen to the frogs if the well dried up?**
   ○ They would have to go back to the swamp.
   ● They would not be able to get out.
   ○ They would not be friends anymore.
   ○ They would not be able to see the bottom.

3. **Read the first paragraph. Which word below means the same as** *prefer*?
   ○ hate
   ○ rehearse
   ○ imagine
   ● like

4. **According to the second frog, why should they think again about the well as a home?**

   Answers will vary. Possible answer:

   The well might dry up. Then they

   might not be able to get out.

5. **Which sentence best expresses the theme of the story?**
   ○ Be kind to others.
   ● Think before you act.
   ○ Two frogs are better than one.
   ○ It's better to give than to receive.

How Jenna Saved Dinnertime

Jenna loved her baby brother Mikey. Every day after school, she would play her harmonica for him. Some of the notes were incorrect, but Mikey didn't care. He always responded by smiling and cooing.

Although Mikey was happy most of the time, he cried almost every night at dinnertime. One night during dinner, Mikey cried so much that his face became red. "What can we do to make him feel better?" Mom asked.

"I know!" Jenna said. She ran and got her harmonica. As soon as she started playing it, Mikey's tears stopped. Then he smiled and fell asleep.

"Jenna, that was amazing!" Mom said.

From that day on, Jenna played the harmonica for Mikey before dinner. Then she and her family ate while Mikey slept peacefully.

© Harcourt

6. Which word describes Mikey's mood most of the time?

○ fussy
● happy
○ hungry
○ bored

7. What does Jenna play for Mikey?

●

○

○

○

8. What is the meaning of *incorrect* as it is used in the first paragraph?

○ able to correct
○ one who corrects
● not correct
○ the state of being correct

9. Which word <u>best</u> describes Jenna?

● smart
○ selfish
○ untalented
○ shy

10. How does dinnertime change for the family?

● Mikey sleeps instead of crying.
○ Jenna plays between bites.
○ Mikey is fussy instead of happy.
○ Mom sleeps instead of making dinner.

A "New" Animal

The year was 1900, and Sir Harry Johnston was in East Africa. He was an explorer. He knew most of the animals of East Africa. He also knew all the animals in the zoos of England. But now he was looking at an animal he had never seen before.

Sir Harry asked the African people about the animal. The people were surprised at his questions. They had always known about this animal. They hunted it for food. They used its skin for leather clothes and bags.

The animal was the okapi. Okapis are related to giraffes. An okapi's neck is long but not as long as a giraffe's neck. A male okapi has short horns. They are covered with skin, just like a giraffe's horns.

An okapi's skin is dark and purplish-brown. The upper parts of its legs have white stripes. The lower parts of its legs may be white or purple. Its face is a lighter color than its body.

An okapi's eyes are large and dark. Its ears are big, and it has a good sense of hearing. An okapi's tongue is very long. The animal can wash its eyes with its tongue!

Okapis eat leaves and seeds. They also eat fruit. Okapis live in thick forests, and they travel around by day. Mostly, they travel alone or with one or two other okapis. They do not travel in herds.

When Sir Harry Johnston returned to England, he told people about the new animal he had "discovered."

11. **Why is the word <u>New</u> in quotation marks in the title of this passage?**
    - ○ because the title looks better that way
    - ○ to show that someone said this word
    - ○ because the animal was surprised
    - ● because the animal was not new to the people of East Africa

12. **What can an okapi do that most animals cannot?**
    - ○ hear very well
    - ○ pick up objects with its hooves
    - ● wash its eyes with its tongue
    - ○ travel in herds

13. **Which of the following words from the passage has a suffix that means "a person who"?**
    - ○ upper
    - ○ mostly
    - ○ lighter
    - ● explorer

14. **What happened <u>after</u> Sir Harry Johnston returned to England?**
    - ○ His boat capsized at sea.
    - ● He told people about his "discovery."
    - ○ He spoke to the African people.
    - ○ He hunted okapis for food.

15. **How is an okapi like a giraffe?**
    - ○ Both have stripes and spots.
    - ● Both have long necks and horns.
    - ○ Both are purple and brown.
    - ○ Both travel in large herds.

16. **Why were the African people surprised at Sir Harry's questions?**
    - ○ They thought he was rude.
    - ● They had always known about the okapi.
    - ○ They didn't know he could talk.
    - ○ They thought he was there to hunt.

STOP

English/Language Arts

1. Which one is <u>not</u> a complete sentence?

- ○ Jake and Tony played a board game.
- ○ The games are kept in the closet.
- ● Several pieces from the games.
- ○ They picked up the pieces and put them away.

2. Read the sentence and choose the correct punctuation mark.

How many times have you played this game before

- ● ?
- ○ .
- ○ !
- ○ ,

STOP

Name _____

1. **Which underlined word is a noun?**
   ○ On weekends she rides <u>her</u> bike.
   ○ The trail <u>winds</u> along the lake.
   ● Many birds make their <u>home</u> there.
   ○ <u>Tall</u> trees provide shade from the sun.

2. **Read the sentence and look at the underlined part. Choose the answer with the correct capital letters and punctuation. If the underlined part is correct, mark "Correct."**

   We had <u>cake ice cream, and</u> punch at the party.

   ● cake, ice cream, and
   ○ cake ice cream and
   ○ cake, ice, cream, and
   ○ Correct

3. **_____ flew to the nearest tree branch.**
   ○ A small black
   ○ One of the
   ● Several blue jays
   ○ At the end of the day

4. **What is the purpose of the sentence below?**

   Put that book on the table.

   ○ make a statement
   ● give a command
   ○ ask a question
   ○ state a strong feeling

5. **What is the complete predicate in the sentence below?**

   The skater won two gold medals at the Olympics.

   ○ The skater won
   ○ won
   ○ won two gold
   ● won two gold medals at the Olympics

6. **Choose the form of the word that best completes the sentence below.**

   Angela will _____ at the parent meeting this Tuesday.

   ● speak
   ○ speaks
   ○ speaking
   ○ spoke

7. Which sentence below is the best closing sentence for the paragraph above?

> At last Wendy's performance was about to begin. She heard the announcer call her name. She walked across the stage to the music stand. Wendy set her music on the stand and cleared her throat. She sang like a songbird, without a single mistake.
> _____

- ○ Wendy has practice every Tuesday and Thursday.
- ○ Wendy liked the fabric of the announcer's dress.
- ○ Wendy needs to study for a spelling test.
- ● Wendy took a bow as the audience clapped loudly.

8. In the sentence below, which pronoun would best replace the underlined words?

The little boy with red hair tossed the ball gently to his friend.

- ○ They
- ○ We
- ● He
- ○ She

9. What type of sentence is the one below?

Wow, what an incredible sunset that is!

- ○ a declarative sentence
- ● an exclamatory sentence
- ○ an interrogative sentence
- ○ an imperative sentence

10. Terry is reading a chapter in her science book about rocks and minerals. She comes across the word metamorphic and is not sure what it means. Where in the book should she look to possibly find the definition of the word metamorphic?

- ○ the table of contents
- ● the glossary
- ○ the copyright page
- ○ the index

11. After the picnic, the children _____.

- ○ on the bus
- ○ later in the afternoon
- ○ to ride horses down the trail
- ● walked back to camp

12. Choose the word that is spelled correctly.

My family _____ eats at the corner restaurant.

- ○ allways
- ● always
- ○ olways
- ○ alweys

13. Choose the word that is the object pronoun in the sentence below.

She quickly passed the paper to me.

- ○ She
- ○ paper
- ○ quickly
- ● me

14. Choose the answer that <u>best</u> replaces the underlined words.

Several children brought cookies to the <u>party</u>.

- ○ him
- ○ them
- ● it
- ○ us

15. In the following sentence, which word is a possessive noun?

The clown's trousers were too big for his legs.

- ● clown's
- ○ trousers
- ○ his
- ○ legs

16. Choose the answer that <u>best</u> describes the sentence below.

I ran fast, but I didn't win the prize.

- ○ an incomplete sentence
- ○ a simple sentence
- ○ a run-on sentence
- ● a compound sentence

17. Look at the sentence in the box. The sentence has two mistakes in capital letters, punctuation, or grammar. Find the two mistakes and correct them. Mark through each mistake or use editing marks. If needed, write the correction above the mistake.

Yesterday, I ask sam to play.

asked; Sam

18. Choose the form of the word that best completes the sentence below.

My sister is a bit _____ than I am.

- ○ more shorter
- ○ more short
- ● shorter
- ○ shortest

19. Which word below is the plural form of the noun <u>woman</u>?

- ○ womans
- ● women
- ○ womens
- ○ womanes

20. Choose the word that is spelled correctly.

The new student is the fastest _____ in our class.

- ○ runer
- ○ runnor
- ● runner
- ○ runor

21. Choose the word that is the adjective in the sentence below.

The cake was placed on a small table by the door.

- ○ cake
- ○ placed
- ● small
- ○ by

22. Choose the sentence that is <u>not</u> written correctly?

- ○ How much money is in your pocket?
- ○ I have three quarters and three dimes.
- ○ That is just the right amount!
- ● Do you have enough change to buy a magazine.

23. Which sentence below is the <u>best</u> topic sentence for the paragraph?

The Indian Paintbrush has crimson petals that wave in the breeze. Thistles have spiky leaves and purple flowers. Blue Cornflowers bask in the bright sunlight. All of these flowers are a sight to see!

- ● In early spring, the meadow is filled with native wildflowers.
- ○ My mom mowed the lawn on Saturday.
- ○ Follow these steps to plant a seed.
- ○ Several people wanted to go for a walk.

24. Which word below is the plural form of the noun <u>berry</u>?

- ● berries
- ○ berrys
- ○ berryes
- ○ berry

© Harcourt

25. Choose the sentence below that is written correctly?

○ This turned out to be the most happiest day of her life.

● This turned out to be the happiest day of her life.

○ This turned out to be the more happier day of her life.

○ This turned out to be the more happy day of her life.

26. Choose the word that is spelled correctly.

A wooden _____ was missing from the front of my sweater.

○ buton

○ buten

○ butten

● button

27. Look at the sentence in the box. The sentence has two mistakes in capital letters, punctuation, or grammar. Find the two mistakes and correct them. Mark through each mistake or use editing marks. If needed, write the correction above the mistake.

> My mother has been a teacher at Thomas Edison high School for six years?

High; change ? to.

28. Choose the answer that best describes a change needed in the sentence below.

Our reports on Native Americans will be due in too weeks.

○ change reports to Reports

○ change be to are

○ change due to dew

● change too to two

29. Robert has been assigned to read Chapter 2 in his history book. He wants to quickly find out what the chapter is about. Where in the book could he look to find out the subject of Chapter 2?

● the table of contents

○ the index

○ the glossary

○ the title page

Choose the simple subject and simple predicate in the sentence below.

30. Many leaves swirled about the dried brown grass.

○ Many/leaves

● eaves/swirled

○ about/grass

○ Many leaves/swirled about

GO ON

31. Choose the sentence with a verb written in the past tense.
- ⭘ The volcano may erupt at any time.
- ⭘ The villagers prepare for that time.
- ⭘ Scientists are studying the volcano.
- ● Several families packed their possessions.

32. Read the sentence and look at the underlined part. Choose the answer with the correct capital letters and punctuation. If the underlined part is correct, mark "Correct."

Susan and i took an evening train into downtown San Diego.
- ● Susan and I
- ⭘ susan and i
- ⭘ Susan, and i
- ⭘ Correct

33. Choose the word that best completes the sentence below.

Theresa and I _____ popcorn before the movie began.
- ⭘ makes
- ● made
- ⭘ making
- ⭘ maked

34. Read the sentence and look at the underlined part. Choose the answer with the correct capital letters and punctuation. If the underlined part is correct, mark "Correct."

This year, my birthday will be on Moday September 23, 2003.
- ⭘ monday September 23, 2003.
- ⭘ Monday September 23, 2003?
- ● Monday, September 23, 2003.
- ⭘ Correct

35. Choose the word that is spelled correctly.

Sarah thought she had _____ a different path back home.
- ⭘ fownd
- ⭘ foond
- ● found
- ⭘ foand

36. Choose the pronoun that best replaces the underlined words.

Please give the papers to Steven and his sister.
- ⭘ they
- ⭘ us
- ⭘ her
- ● them

GO ON

Name _____

37. Choose the <u>best</u> topic sentence for the paragraph.

> The first thing in the morning, we boarded the bus. Once we arrived, we divided into small groups. We spent the next three hours looking at the exhibits. After that, we ate our bag lunches. Finally, it was time to go home.

- ○ Dinosaurs lived long ago.
- ○ My class held a science fair.
- ● Today was our field trip to the natural history museum.
- ○ I packed a sandwich and an apple in my lunch.

38. Choose the word that is spelled correctly.

Her grandmother _____ water in a teakettle on the stove.

- ● boiled
- ○ boyled
- ○ boyld
- ○ boilt

39. Which sentence below is <u>not</u> a complete sentence?

- ● A fascinating story about two mice in the country.
- ○ We read the book several times.
- ○ I read the comic and gave it to Sherry.
- ○ Sherry spent her money on gum and a bookmark.

40. Choose the words that <u>best</u> complete the sentence below.

I could see that _____ little mice had made a nest under the _____ deck.

- ● eight, new
- ○ eight, knew
- ○ ate, knew
- ○ ate, new

41. Choose the word that <u>best</u> completes the sentence below.

Mom took my _____ coat to the cleaners yesterday.

- ○ sisters
- ● sister's
- ○ sisteres
- ○ sisters's

42. Look at the sentence in the box. The sentence has two mistakes in capital letters, punctuation, or grammar. Find the two mistakes and correct them. Mark through each mistake or use editing marks. If needed, write the correction above the mistake.

> The next part of the Play are really exciting.

play; change are to is

STOP